Exercises in Critical Thinking

Thinking

·······It·······

Through

OMMUNITY

GLOBE FEARON
EDUCATIONAL PUBLISHER
PARAMUS, NEW JERSEY

Paramount Publishing

Executive Editor: Barbara Levadi
Editor: Carol Schneider
Editorial Assistant: Roger Weisman
Product Development: Cynthia Benjamin, Frank Puccio,
    and Sandra Sella Raas
Art Director: Nancy Sharkey
Designer: Joan Jacobus
Production Director: Penny Gibson
Manufacturing Supervisor: Della Smith
Senior Production Editor: Linda Greenberg
Production Editor: Alan Dalgleish
Marketing Manager: Sandra Hutchison
Photo Research: Jenifer Hixson
Electronic Page Supervision and Production: Margarita Giammanco
Electronic Page Production: Maria Falkenberg, Joan Jacobus,
    José López, and Luc Van Meerbeek
Cover Design: Design Five

Globe Fearon Educational Publisher wishes to thank the following copyright owners
for permission to reproduce illustrations and photographs in this book:
p. 5: Andrea M. Vuocolo; **p. 7**: UPI/Bettmann Newsphotos;
p. 19: Laurie Harden; **p. 33**: Joe Veno; **p. 35**: UPI/Bettmann Newsphotos;
p. 49: Tom Barrett; **p. 50** and **51**: William Negron;
p. 65: Tom Barrett; **p. 68**: Marvin Friedman;
p. 81: Laurie Harden; **p. 82**: Steve and Mary Beran Skjold;
p. 83: Steve and Mary Beran Skjold; **p. 84**: Steve and Mary Beran Skjold.

Printed in the United States of America
1 2 3 4 5 6 7 8 9 10   99 98 97 96 95 94

ISBN: 0-835-90918-2

GLOBE FEARON
EDUCATIONAL PUBLISHER
PARAMUS, NEW JERSEY

Paramount Publishing

CONTENTS

UNIT 1

Thinking About Citizenship

CIVIL rights are the building blocks of a free society. They are the rights that people enjoy as citizens of a country. The Constitution defines those basic rights for all U.S. citizens. It states, for example, that all people should be able to live their lives in freedom and be able to seek happiness.

The first ten amendments to the Constitution, called the Bill of Rights, list the specific rights and freedoms that citizens of the United States have. You will learn about these rights in Lesson 1.

In this unit, you will think critically about civil rights and will express your opinion about what they are and whom they are for. You will make evaluations about which rights are most important to you and to the community in which you live. You will also examine your attitudes about other people and their rights.

You will then turn your attention to other issues of citizenship in the United States. You will analyze how these issues are interpreted and shown in television programs and movies. You will also discuss majority and minority groups and will support your opinions about issues of fairness and equality in your own school and community.

For the unit project, you will research issues surrounding the right to own and keep weapons. You will then participate in a discussion about this controversial issue and will propose other solutions to violence.

5

Thurgood Marshall:

Thurgood Marshall died in 1993 at the age of 84. His public funeral at the National Cathedral in Washington, D.C., drew more mourners than any national figure since President John F. Kennedy. More than 19,000 people of all races and from all walks of life, including public servants, judges, law clerks, politicians, civil-rights leaders, entertainers, teachers, and school children, came to pay their respects to Marshall.

Marshall was born on July 2, 1908, in Baltimore, Maryland. His great-grandfather had been brought to this same city as a slave from Africa. Marshall's mother was an elementary-school teacher and his father was a train-car porter. His parents believed that giving their son a good education would teach him to stand up for his rights as a citizen of the United States.

The Early Years

Every day after school, Marshall's father would question him about his schoolwork. Marshall believed that these "question-and-answer" sessions helped him to think like a lawyer. Marshall's father would make him prove every point with sound logic and reasons.

After graduating from Lincoln University, an all-black college, as a predental student, Marshall decided to become a lawyer. He applied to the University of Maryland Law School, an all-white school, but was rejected because of his race. Although this prejudice was not unusual at that time, Marshall remembered it all of his life. But this incident did not stop him. Marshall applied to Howard University Law School and was accepted. He graduated in 1933 at the top of his class.

When Marshall started practicing law, the country was in the middle of the Great Depression. Millions of people were unemployed and money was scarce. Marshall decided to provide legal services for people who could least afford them. As a result, he quickly and fondly became known as "the little man's lawyer."

Helping African Americans

Marshall became a lawyer for the NAACP (National Association for the Advancement of Colored People) and worked on issues of civil rights for African Americans. He traveled all over the country during the 1930s and 1940s seeking the rights of African Americans to vote, buy homes, and attend elementary schools and state colleges. He won his first case in 1934 when he convinced a state court to admit the first black student to the University of Maryland Law School—the same school that rejected him only five years earlier.

Thurgood Marshall continued to be concerned about the "separate-but-equal" law that was responsible for keeping black children and white children in separate schools. In 1954, the Supreme Court ruled that this law was unconstitutional and directed the desegregation of all public schools in

America. This monumental change in the federal law was the result of Marshall's work.

In 1961, Marshall was appointed as a circuit-court judge. Six years later, he became a Supreme Court justice. Marshall was the ninety-sixth man and the first African American to sit on the Supreme Court. He served on the Court for 25 years.

Marshall was a well-spoken man with a quick wit. Unlike many national figures, he did not surround himself with advisers and press people. He also turned down many book offers, awards, and tributes. When asked why he shied away from special attention and recognition, he would look surprised. "I'm just committed," he often said proudly. "Some things you just don't compromise."

Marshall was a man who made a difference. He argued his convictions without bitterness and violence. His attitude alone was an inspiration to many, considering the violent and emotional times in which he lived.

Eyewitness

Linda Brown Buckner was eight years old in 1951 when her father included her in a lawsuit to desegregate public schools in Topeka, Kansas. Topeka had 22 elementary schools—18 for whites and 4 for blacks. "The closest school to my family was four blocks away, the Sumner School," Linda recalls. "But I went to Monroe Elementary School, which was two-and-a-half miles across town. Often I came home crying because it was so cold waiting for the bus." So Linda's parents joined the fight to desegregate schools in America. In 1954, they won that fight with the Supreme Court's decision in the Brown v. Board of Education case. Linda was in junior high school that year.

Timeline

1896 *Plessy v. Ferguson:* The Supreme Court establishes "separate-but-equal" schools in America.
1954 *Brown v. Board of Education:* The Supreme Court orders the desegregation of schools in America.
1965 Desegregation is established in approximately 38 percent of all Southern school districts.

Lesson 1:
Evaluating Your Civil Rights

THE BILL OF RIGHTS IN BRIEF

1. freedoms of religion, speech, press, assembly, and petition

2. the right to have weapons

3. freedom from military occupation of private homes or property in time of peace

4. freedom from unreasonable search and seizure

5. freedom from self-incrimination and right of equal access to our legal system (due process of law)

6. right to a trial by jury

7. safeguards in lawsuits involving property

8. freedom from excessive fines or bail and from cruel and unusual punishment

9. assurance of personal rights set forth in the Constitution

10. assurance of government powers set forth in the Constitution

Civil rights are the privileges and freedoms that citizens of a country enjoy. Read over the ones listed in the sidenote. These are some of the basic privileges that citizens of the United States have.

Often people do not really understand or appreciate their civil rights until those rights are denied. Read again the list of rights in the sidenote on this page. Then respond to each question below.

1. What does the term *civil rights* mean to you? Give some examples.

_____

_____

_____

2. Which rights do you think are most important in a free society? Why? _____

_____

_____

3. Are some rights more important to you than other rights? Explain.

_____

_____

_____

4. Do you have any rights that you would be willing to give up? If not, why not? If so, which ones? _____

_____

_____

_____

The term *civil rights* is also used to refer to the rights of a minority group to equal, or the same, treatment as a majority group. For example, the Civil Rights Movement of the 1950s and 1960s was a campaign to achieve equality for African Americans in the United States. In this campaign, a minority group demanded the same rights and freedoms that the majority group possessed.

Take an inventory of your opinions about civil rights and equal treatment of people. Check whether you agree or disagree with each statement below.

	AGREE	DISAGREE
1. People should be allowed to express their ideas whether others agree with them or not.		
2. It's OK if my friends have opinions that are different from mine.		
3. Men and women should be treated equally.		
4. People who have the same religious beliefs should live in the same communities.		
5. People of French ancestry should not be paid as much money for their work as people of Japanese ancestry.		
6. It's OK to dislike people whose physical appearance and speech are different from yours.		

As a class, count the number of "agrees" and "disagrees" for each statement. Write the number in each box. Then discuss the results. Which questions were close in the number of "agrees" and "disagrees"? What were some of the majority opinions? What were some of the minority opinions?

DISCUSSION

In 1955, Rosa Parks refused to give up her bus seat to a white man. Her action was one of the first to protest prejudice and segregation in the South. Thirty-eight years later, in 1993, she was interviewed about how the country had changed since the day on which she kept her seat on that bus. "Today we can register to vote, vote, and hold office," she said. "Regretfully, we cannot say all is well with race relations. It appears that racial unrest is on the increase among young adults. We still have a lot of work to do."

Do you think that what she says about racial unrest is true today? Is it true in your community? If your answer is yes, why do you think racial prejudice still exists? What can be done to reduce prejudices?

THE LANGUAGE OF THINKING

To evaluate something is to judge it or to determine its worth or value. Making evaluations requires careful thinking. It is a process that includes weighing all sides before forming a judgment. For example, in this lesson you are being asked to evaluate your civil rights by making a personal judgment about their value. To do this, you might ask yourself questions about how your life is affected by a certain right or freedom. Think carefully about the answers. The answers will help you form a judgment.

Evaluation

Use the following questions to help you evaluate your performance on this lesson.

❑ What did I discover about my personal or civil rights that I hadn't thought about before?

❑ How could I have expressed my thoughts or ideas more clearly in this lesson?

❑ What did I find difficult about this lesson? How did I overcome this difficulty?

Lesson 2:
Analyzing Pictures in the Media

THE LANGUAGE OF THINKING

Analyzing is part of the learning process. When you analyze something, you break it into its parts in order to examine it more closely. When you analyze information, you break it apart in order to think about facts or details more critically and deeply. Analyzing information allows you to categorize and label things. It also allows you to understand situations or issues better.

TV NEWS BLITZ

In 1963, communication satellites made it possible to transmit coverage of events as they were happening around the world.

With this new capability, it became almost impossible for people to ignore what was happening in the world. However, with this ability to reach other parts of the world, the media has a responsibility to the viewing public to represent people fairly and accurately.

Citizenship gives people rights and privileges. It also gives them duties and responsibilities. For example, Americans have the right to a trial by a jury of their fellow citizens. As adults, Americans also have the responsibility to serve as members of those juries.

Exercising your rights and taking responsibility for them is part of the daily life of every American citizen. This focus on civic responsibility is evident not only in the governmental and justice systems, but also in television, newspapers, classrooms, and neighborhoods.

Do programs and movies fairly represent what life is like in the United States? How well are people's rights and responsibilities shown in television programs and in the movies? Do they show people exercising their rights and freedoms? Do they show people being treated equally? Do they show people being responsible citizens?

In the chart below, list the names of television programs that you watch or movies that you have seen recently. Think about the stories, the characters, and the topics covered. Then identify any rights and responsibilities involved. For example, if you watched a situation comedy, did any of the situations involve people being treated unequally or unfairly? If so, how was the problem resolved? If you watched a television program or movie about law enforcement or the courts, did the characters act fairly and responsibly?

	RIGHTS	RESPONSIBILITIES
TV Programs		
Movies		

Go back to your chart and review the titles you listed. Then star those programs or movies that you think did a good job of showing real-life issues of citizenship.

1. Choose one of the starred programs or movies and explain why you starred it. _____

_____

_____

2. What was wrong with, or missing from, the programs or movies that you did not star? Choose one of these titles and explain why you did not give it a star. _____

_____

_____

Impressions about fairness and equality are sometimes formed simply from the photographs that newspapers and magazines run. Sometimes these pictures can be accurate, but sometimes they can be misleading. These photographs can cause people, often without their awareness, to form opinions or biases about other people or about events.

Look through your daily newspaper or a weekly news magazine. Study a few of the photographs. Then read the articles that they illustrate. Do the photographs fairly represent the articles? Do any of them imply something that is not true or fair? How often do you think people form opinions about something just by looking at photographs and not by reading the articles? Do you think that the media has a responsibility to the public to show accurate portrayals of people? With one or two classmates, talk about these questions. Then summarize your findings below.

_____

_____

_____

_____

_____

Evaluation

Use the following questions to help you evaluate your performance on this lesson.

❏ Was I able to think of appropriate issues for the television programs and movies that I watched? If not, what could I have done to make this task easier?

❏ Have I changed any of my attitudes about the rights and responsibilities of citizens? If so, what has changed and why?

Lesson 3:
Examining and Supporting Your Opinions

SUPPORTING IDEAS AND OPINIONS

You know that it is important to use facts and details to support the main ideas in your writing. The quality of your writing depends on such skill. It is also important to use sound reasons and examples to support your opinions. The quality of your thinking also depends on these skills. Take time to think through an opinion and be prepared to give reasons and examples to support it.

A CASE IN POINT

Female athletes and their coaches at Colorado State University had tried for many years to get the university to reinstate the women's softball team. Such a team existed for men. Finally, the athletes filed a lawsuit claiming that the university's sports program was not treating men and women equally. As a result, a federal judge ordered the university to reinstate the women's team.

Protecting your right to equal and fair treatment is an important responsibility. One way in which you protect this right is through education. Once you have learned about your rights, you are better able to defend them. But when it becomes necessary, you can also protect your rights by going to court.

The term *civil rights* includes issues related to minority groups. Today's society is more sensitive not only to differences in race and religion among people, but also to differences in age, gender, physical ability, and sexual preference.

We all belong to a majority group at some times and a minority group at other times. For example, if you were the only male counselor at a summer camp for girls, then you would be in the minority. If you were one of the only three English-speaking people in your classroom, then you would be in the minority.

When have you been in the minority? Write your definition of a minority group below and give some examples.

_____

_____

_____

_____

Count the number of girls and boys that are present in your classroom today. Record the number of each on the lines provided.

Girls _____   Boys _____

Which group is in the majority? _____

Which group is in the minority? _____

In your opinion, are girls and boys treated equally in your classes? Give reasons and examples to support your opinion.

_____

_____

_____

_____

12

Congress has passed many acts and bills in order to enforce equal rights in the United States. For example, Title IX of the Education Amendments, passed in 1972, orders that all schools and colleges treat men and women equally.

Many schools have been criticized for not enforcing the Title IX law in their sports programs. In fact, many cases are waiting to be brought to court to force schools to provide equal athletic opportunities, facilities, and scholarships for men and women. Read the sidenote "A Case in Point" on page 12 for an example of women who fought for equal rights in college athletics.

Think about the sports programs in your school or in your community. Do they offer the same opportunities for both boys and girls?

Write a letter that expresses your opinion about this issue. The letter may either support or criticize a sports program or policy. You may write to your teacher, your physical-education instructor, a coach, or an athletic director. Use the space below to outline the reasons and examples that you will use in your letter. Then write the letter on a separate sheet of paper.

_____

_____

_____

_____

_____

_____

DISCUSSION

In 1989, two teens in Houston, Texas, were suspended from high school until they cut their hair. Both teens were boys. One boy's hair hung to the middle of his back; the other's hung almost to his waist. The school district had a policy that banned boys from wearing their hair past their shoulders. The local school board supported this policy and refused to lift the suspension until the boys got haircuts. The members of the board argued that it is important to learn to follow rules and regulations.

What do you think the boys should have done? Do you think the policy is a form of gender discrimination? Explain your answer.

Evaluation

Use the following questions to help you evaluate your performance on this lesson.

❑ Did I understand the questions and activities? If not, what could I have done to solve this problem?

❑ Was I able to think of a good example of either classroom discrimination or equality to write about? Why was it a good example?

❑ Did I listen respectfully to the opinions of others? If not, how could I improve my listening skills?

Controlling Guns in the Community

In Lesson 1, you reviewed several basic rights that citizens of the United States possess. One of these basic rights is the right to own and keep weapons. But people today have access to a greater variety of weapons, and these weapons are much more powerful than the rifles and pistols that were available when the Bill of Rights was signed.

In Lesson 2, you learned that having rights also means having responsibilities. In Lesson 3, you considered a social issue in our world today—equality between men and women, especially in sports programs. For the unit project, you'll consider another important issue of our modern world—gun control.

For this project, you and your classmates will research current laws and policies and arguments for and against gun control. After sharing your findings, you'll participate in a discussion about the pros and cons of gun control. You'll then work with your classmates to develop a proposal that supports the majority position on gun control.

STEP 1 Researching and Gathering Information..........................

Decide which one of these three groups you wish to join:

Group 1 will research the current laws about buying and owning a gun in your city, town, or state.

Group 2 will research the arguments in favor of gun control.

Group 3 will research the arguments against gun control.

With the members of your group, brainstorm possible issues for your topic. Take time to think of and discuss as many ideas as you can. Use the following graphic organizer to help you organize your group's ideas and suggestions. It might be helpful to phrase your issues as questions.

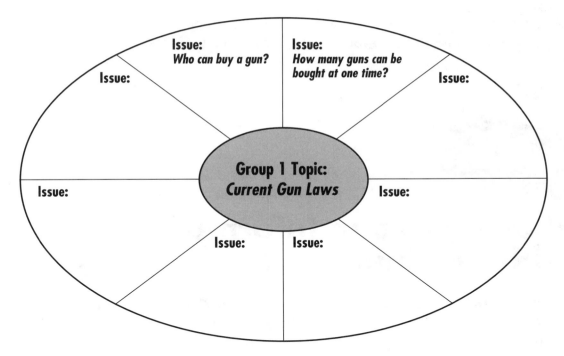

Using the graphic organizer as a guide, decide as a group for which issues each member will be responsible. Then begin researching your topic to find information about your assigned issue.

Use a variety of sources in your research, such as newspapers, magazines, brochures, news programs, and personal interviews. A librarian can help you find current information about gun control. News programs often report information about gun-control laws and statistics about gun purchases and ownership. Interviewing people who work in law enforcement and owners of stores that sell guns can also provide valuable information.

STEP 2

Sharing Information within Your Group...................

Take turns presenting the results of your individual research to the members of your group. As each member is speaking, listen carefully and take notes about any new information that is presented.

Then as a group, make a list of the main points of the topic that your group researched. Be sure to list a point only once. After the list is completed, review it to make sure that all of the important points are listed.

*R*eview your group's list and star at least three main points that you will make about your topic. Then choose one member to present the main points of the topic to the class.

Sharing Group Information with the Class...

Representatives from the three groups will now share the main points of their gun control topics with everyone. This sharing of information will enable all students to learn about the results of the research done by all three groups.

*T*o begin, a representative from Group 1 will present information about current gun laws. A representative from Group 2 will present the main arguments in favor of gun control, and one from Group 3 will present the main arguments against gun control. Listen carefully and critically to the information presented by all of the groups. Fill in the following graphic organizer with reasons for and against gun control laws as each group presents its findings.

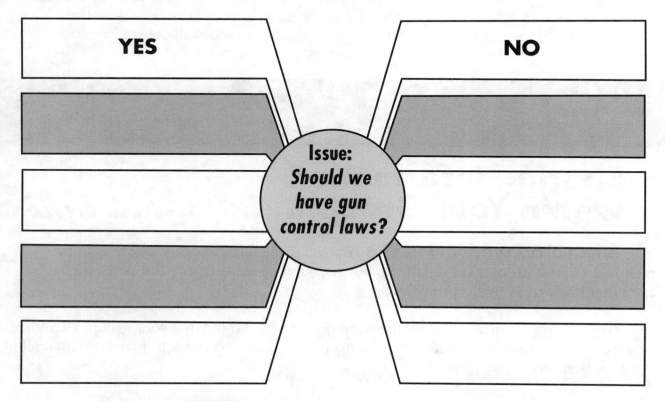

YES

NO

Issue:
Should we
have gun
control laws?

Conducting an Open Class Discussion......................................

All students should now have the necessary facts and information about gun control. As a group of informed citizens, draw from your knowledge to discuss the following questions:

- Are the current laws and policies adequate?
- Should we have gun-control laws?
- How could the current laws and policies be more effective?

As a class, agree on an answer to each of the three questions. Keep in mind that the majority opinion should be represented in the answers to the questions.

Then develop a class proposal that supports the majority opinion for the third question above. Be sure to list specific reasons and give examples in the proposal.

Look at several different letters to the editor published in your local magazines and your local newspapers. Using these examples, write your class proposal in the form of a letter to the editor. Be sure that someone calls the newspaper first to find out how such a letter should be submitted.

STEP 5 *Evaluating What You Have Learned*......................................

Consider what you knew about gun control before you began your research. Did you change your mind about this issue because of this project? If people knew more about the facts and issues of gun control, do you think we would have better laws? In small groups or as a class, talk about your answers to these questions.

Then individually determine your grade for the project based on your contributions and participation in group discussions and in the writing of the class proposal.

UNIT 1 TEST

1. Circle the letter that correctly completes the statement. Explain your choice on the lines provided.

   It is important to be an active and informed citizen because citizens
   a. have responsibilities to protect their rights.
   b. are responsible only for themselves.
   c. can never change their opinions about issues.

   _____
   _____
   _____

Answer the following question on the lines provided. Support your answer with examples and details.

2. Describe the ways in which you are an active citizen, or the ways in which you can become a more active citizen in your community.

   _____
   _____
   _____
   _____
   _____
   _____
   _____
   _____
   _____

Answer the following essay question on a separate sheet of paper. Support your answer with examples and details.

3. Technology has often been accused of jeopardizing people's personal and civil rights. For example, some people say that hidden cameras in public places violate their rights of privacy. Bank and store managers, however, argue that these cameras are necessary in order to help prevent crime and to apprehend criminals. What do you think? Should hidden cameras be allowed in public places?

18

UNIT 2

Decision Making in a Democracy

BEING part of a community means that you enjoy certain rights, but with these rights come responsibility. Voting is an important responsibility for all citizens living in a community.

The leaders of our communities, states, and nation are selected through an election process. Americans are not required to vote, but they all have the opportunity. When Americans decide not to vote, they are giving the message that they have little interest in whom their leaders will be.

Did you ever wonder what it would be like to live in a country that does not elect its leaders? To most Americans, this is an unthinkable idea. But the citizens of many countries do not have the privilege of voting.

In this unit, you'll think critically about how one becomes an educated voter. You'll compare and contrast the viewpoints of two candidates running for a political office. You'll decide which of the candidates you like better and which personal qualities you think are important for political candidates. You'll also take a look at why voting is so important at the community level by exploring a community issue. You'll read about two opposing points of view concerning a community issue, and then you'll be asked to cast a vote on this issue.

As a unit project, you'll follow a recently held state or local election to see democracy in action.

PULL TO CLOSE CURTAIN

LOOK, LISTEN AND VOTE!

"Good evening. This is Janet Edwards for WXYZ, Channel 5 News, bringing you the latest on tomorrow's important election. Everyone is predicting that this will be the closest election in years. The candidates have campaigned long and hard to bring their ideas before the people.

"As you all know, one of the ways candidates get their ideas across is by using slogans. These slogans can be read on billboards all over your community. They can be heard on the radio and can be seen on television commercials. How much impact do you think these short but catchy slogans have on the voter? Probably more than you think. Let's take a minute to look back on each candidate's most successful campaign slogans."

(On the television screen flashes three slogans urging citizens to vote for challenger Charlotte Smith.)

**A VOTE FOR
CHARLOTTE SMITH
IS A VOTE FOR OUR FUTURE!**

**CHARLOTTE SMITH. . .
NEW IDEAS,
NEW BEGINNINGS!**

**OUR CHILDREN
DESERVE BETTER . . .
VOTE FOR CHARLOTTE SMITH**

(Then three campaign slogans for Jack Johnson are shown.)

**VOTE FOR JACK JOHNSON . . .
LET'S KEEP A GOOD THING
GOING!**

**JACK JOHNSON . . . LET'S FINISH
WHAT WE STARTED**

**A REASON TO HOPE . . . RE-ELECT
JACK JOHNSON**

"The candidates' messages come through loud and clear in their slogans. The challenger, Charlotte Smith, is telling voters that a change in leadership is needed,

WHY I WOULD ☆VOTE FOR☆ CHARLOTTE SMITH

- ☒ She will initiate change in our community.
- ☒ She will bring more jobs into our community.
- ☒ She will improve our schools.
- ☒ She will make our neighborhood streets safer.

☆

whereas Jack Johnson is trying to convince voters that he needs another term in office to complete the work he has started. What do you think? Did these slogans influence how you are going to vote in tomorrow's election?

"Campaign slogans don't tell the whole story of this election. To really understand what each candidate stands for, we must get a complete picture of what they plan to do if elected. To achieve this goal, it is necessary for everyone to listen critically to what each candidate is saying. Let's go live to listen in on each candidate's final campaign speech."

(On screen is Charlotte Smith concluding a speech to a group of citizens at an outdoor rally.)

". . . It has been a long, hard campaign. I believe that you, the voters, understand the differences between Mr. Johnson and me. As you enter the voting booth tomorrow, I ask that you remember the hard times that we have all been through over the past four years. The high unemployment rates, the increased drop-out rate in our schools, and the rise of drug and alcohol abuse by our young people. We must put an end to these problems. A vote for Charlotte Smith is a vote for more jobs, better schools, and safer streets. Thank you for your support!"

(Viewers are switched directly to the campaign headquarters of Jack Johnson, who is speaking to some of his supporters.)

". . . We have come to the end of a long and difficult road. My opponent has made many promises during the campaign. But I can show you proof of the progress we have made over the past four years. Businesses and jobs are beginning to move back into our communities. Tests scores are

★ ★ ★ ★ ★ ★ ★
WHY I WOULD VOTE FOR JACK JOHNSON
★ ★ ★

- ☒ **He has done a good job the last 4 years.**
- ☒ **He has brought jobs to our community.**
- ☒ **He has improved our schools.**
- ☒ **He has increased the number of police on our streets.**

improving in our schools. The addition of police officers on our streets is beginning to have an effect on the sale and use of illegal drugs. I believe that we are heading in the right direction and with your vote tomorrow, we can continue our programs. Let's keep a good thing going!"

(The screen flashes back to Janet Edwards, who is standing outside the Johnson campaign headquarters.)

"Tonight the campaign ends. No more slogans or speeches. It is this reporter's opinion that both candidates have successfully brought their ideas before the people. Although there are similarities between Ms. Smith and Mr. Johnson, there are even more differences. Their plans to create more jobs, to improve our schools, and to combat drugs are as different as night and day.

"Now it's up to the voters. Don't let the opportunity pass you by—vote for the candidate of your choice! This is Janet Edwards. Good night and good news!"

Lesson 1:
Comparing and Contrasting Political Candidates

THE LANGUAGE OF THINKING

Comparing and contrasting means looking for similarities and differences. It is an important skill to learn when making choices. You practice this skill daily.

For example, when was the last time you went shopping for a new pair of sneakers and had a difficult time choosing between two or more pairs? By comparing and contrasting, you made a decision.

POLITICAL PLATFORMS

During elections, you often hear the term **platform**. This word refers to the set of policies that a candidate or political party hopes to put into action if elected. Each individual part of the platform is known as a plank. For example, a plank in a candidate's or party's platform might be to lower taxes.

". . . and when I am elected the governor of your fine state, I promise to . . ."

How many times have political candidates made this statement? But how closely do people listen to what is being said? To make informed decisions about whom they should vote for, voters need to know each candidate's platform. They also need to listen critically to what political candidates are saying.

Below are parts of speeches given by two candidates running for state governor. Read each candidate's statement. Then use the Venn diagram on the next page to show how the two candidates agree and disagree on this topic.

CANDIDATE A

Over the past few years, our state's education system has had to deal with some very serious problems. First, our test scores have steadily declined. Second, we have the highest student-to-teacher ratio in the country. Third, violence is increasing in all our schools.

Let me explain to you how I plan to improve education in our state. We need to improve the technology available in our schools. I will make sure that every school in our state is equipped with state-of-the-art learning technology. I will ask the state legislature for money to build additional schools and to hire more teachers. And, I will get tough on violence in our schools. Students carrying weapons into schools will be arrested.

To carry out my plans, some new taxes may be necessary. I promise, however, that none of these new taxes will affect your personal income. Your vote for me in the upcoming election will help me make our state a leader in public education.

CANDIDATE B

The education system of our great state is in need of a "shot in the arm." After years of leading the nation, our students are struggling to compete. Changes are needed to get us back to where we once were. To achieve this goal, I plan to do three things. First, I would like every school in our state to have a computer lab equipped with the most up-to-date equipment. Second, I plan to have armed guards on duty in schools that are experiencing problems with drugs and violence. Repeat drug and weapons offenders will be expelled. Third, I plan to give parents more choice in their children's education. Under my plan, parents can send their children to the public or private school of their choice. This plan will not only help every student, but it will also create better schools.

The best thing about my plans to improve our education system is that no new taxes will be needed. So, remember, a vote for me in next week's election will be a vote for real change in our education system.

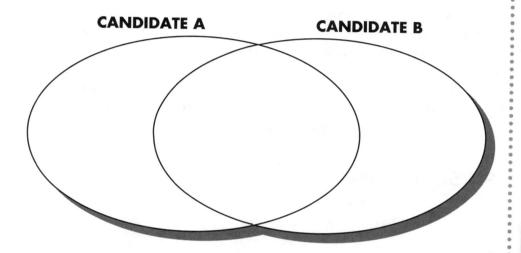

CANDIDATE A   **CANDIDATE B**

After you have completed the Venn diagram, answer the following questions.

1. What are the differences between the two candidates' plans to improve education?_____
_____
_____

2. What do you think is missing from each candidate's plan?
_____
_____

3. Which candidate has the better plan for improving education? Why?_____
_____
_____

Evaluation
●●●●●●●●●

Use the following questions to help you evaluate your performance on this lesson.

❑ What process did I use to find the similarities and differences between the two candidates? Was this process effective? Why or why not?

❑ How did the diagram help me to compare the candidates?

❑ Was I able to support my choice of a candidate? Why or why not?

Lesson 2:
Making Decisions about Political Candidates

Making decisions requires a number of skills. To make successful decisions, you must be able to do the following:

❏ identify the problem

❏ gather and analyze information

❏ propose several solutions or options

❏ compare and contrast your solutions or options

❏ form and test possible solutions

❏ reach a decision

DESCRIPTIVE WORDS

The following are some words that you might consider including in your description:

bold

global-minded

determined

persuasive

compassionate

Citizens in a democracy elect their political leaders. As a result, every citizen must not only know how each candidate stands on issues, but must also know each candidate's personal qualities. Before casting a vote for a candidate, ask yourself the following questions:

- Do I agree with this candidate on the issues?
- Does this candidate have the personal qualities that I would like my elected leaders to have?

Below is a list of personal qualities. Rank each quality from 1 to 10, with 1 being the most important personal quality that a political leader should possess and 10 being the least important.

PERSONAL QUALITIES

_____ modesty

_____ common sense

_____ sense of humor

_____ ability to create new ideas

_____ ability to make decisions

_____ loyalty

_____ courage

_____ determination

_____ honesty

_____ morality

On a separate sheet of paper write a one-paragraph description of your ideal political candidate.

Select a political candidate or elected official you like. Read about this person in several articles from local, city, and national publications. As you read the articles, fill in the following chart with issues and personal qualities that are discussed or described in the articles. In the columns next to Issues, check whether you agree or disagree with the person's position. In the column next to Qualities, check whether the quality is positive or negative. Then answer the questions that follow.

Issues	Agree	Disagree	Qualities	+	-

1. Do you think the articles you read about your chosen political leader or elected official were accurate? Why or why not?_____

_____

_____

2. Does the person have the personal qualities you would like elected leaders to have? Why or why not?_____

_____

_____

3. Would you still vote for the person if you could? Why or why not? _____

_____

_____

DISCUSSION

During a recent political campaign, a candidate's personal life received much attention. Some people believe that a candidate's personal life is his or her own business and has no effect on a candidate's ability to carry out the duties of an elected official. Others believe that a candidate's personal life will be reflected in the decisions that he or she makes. Would you vote for a candidate whose personal life does not measure up to your expectations? Should a candidate's personal life be "off limits" even if he or she is running for a public office?

Lesson 3:
Prioritizing Goals for a Community

THE LANGUAGE OF THINKING

To prioritize simply means to put in order of importance. Put the most important thing first, the next important thing second, and so on.

We prioritize in many areas of our lives. For example, have you ever had too many things to do in one day, and you knew that you would never get all of them done? You had to decide which activities absolutely had to get done first and which could wait until later. When you go through this process, you are prioritizing.

Pottersville is a tiny farming community located in the middle of a large agricultural state. For the last five years, this quiet community has been invaded by the hustle and bustle of the 1990s. Pottersville's traffic, noise, and visitors have increased because of two highways that have been built around the town.

In the northwest corner of Pottersville is a large piece of land that is home to thousands of birds. Bird-watchers from all over the state bring their cameras and video recorders, hoping to capture these beautiful birds on film.

At a recent town meeting, Mr. Johnson, one of Pottersville's newest residents, made a proposal to use this land to build a shopping mall. "After all," Mr. Johnson said, "Pottersville is changing. The new mall will help meet the needs of the townspeople. In addition, it will create many new jobs and will attract shoppers from nearby towns."

Many long-time residents of Pottersville are very upset. What will happen to the birds? They argue that the birds have been on this land long before Pottersville even existed.

Mr. Johnson, however, did not back down. "The bird-watchers," he said, "make up a very small part of the town's population. A much larger number of people will use and enjoy the mall. The money the town raises in taxes can be used to build new parks and playgrounds in other parts of town. Pottersville must be willing to change if the city is to grow!" The town council agreed to put the issue to vote during the next election.

Imagine that you are a citizen of Pottersville. How would you vote? Use the following table to prioritize points made by both sides of the argument.

Home for Birds	New Shopping Mall

26

1. I would vote to _____

_____

_____.

2. The reason I would vote this way is _____

_____

_____

_____.

Holding a Class Debate

3. What are some local issues that are being decided by members

of your community?_____

_____

_____

_____.

Select one issue that is being decided in your community. Hold a class debate about that issue. As a class, determine each side of the issue and record these on a chalkboard or poster. Then divide into groups according to your position on the issue.

As a group, create a statement that defends your point of view. That statement will be read to the class by a spokesperson. After all the statements have been read, present a rebuttal. During the rebuttal, try to disprove the other groups' arguments. At the end of the rebuttal, make your group's final points, or closing argument. Conclude the debate by writing a statement that incorporates the best arguments from all sides that were represented.

DISCUSSION

The small percentage of people who vote in state and local elections has become a major problem in the United States. People give reasons for not voting, such as a lack of interest, a distrust of politics and politicians, or a feeling that one vote will not make a difference. Why is it important that a person living in a democracy vote? How might teens try to increase the number of voters in their community?

BOOKSHELF

You can find many resources in a library or bookstore about citizenship and voting. The following are just a few of the books that are available. Check with your teacher, librarian, or a local bookstore owner for more titles.

Responsibility, by Glenn Alan Cheney.

Civics: Citizens and Society, by Allan O. Kownslar and Terry L. Smart.

Election Night, by Thomas Raber.

Voting and Elections, by Dennis B. Fradin.

Evaluation

Use the following questions to help you evaluate your performance on this lesson.

❑ What did I learn about understanding all sides of an issue?

❑ What citizenship skills did I learn about in this lesson?

❑ What can I do to prepare myself to make informed decisions when I vote?

Taking a Closer Look at Political Elections

Citizens living in a democracy have the right to vote. Voting for political leaders is an important responsibility that every American has. But to be a responsible voter, people must know the issues and the candidates.

In Lesson 1, you learned how to compare and contrast the viewpoints of political candidates. In Lesson 2, you made decisions concerning the personal qualities that you want to see in a political candidate. In Lesson 3, you were asked to look at a community issue, analyze the arguments, and make a personal decision concerning the issue.

For the unit project, you'll look at democracy and citizenship in action. You'll study a recent state or local election. You'll research the candidates, issues, public opinions, and election outcome. In an oral presentation you'll share your findings with the class.

STEP 1   Researching Background Information..........................

With a small group of students, select a recently held election in your community or state. Then research the backgrounds of the candidates who took part in that election. Create a personal profile poster for each candidate by completing the following :

1. Candidate's Name: _____

2. Hometown: _____

3. Present Residence: _____

4. College/University: _____

5. Degrees Earned: _____

6. Previous Political Offices Held: _____

Analyzing the Issues........................

Next, you must find out what issues were debated during the campaign. Then find out each candidate's opinion on each issue. This information can be found in newspapers and magazines that were published during the campaign. If the election received television coverage, you may be able to get video clips of speeches made by the candidates during the campaign. Once you have gathered this information, use the table below to help you to analyze each candidate's position on the issues. In the left-hand column, list the issues. In the right-hand column, summarize the candidate's position each issue. Create a separate table for each candidate.

Candidate's Name:	
Issues	Candidate's Position

Identifying Public Opinion..............

Next, conduct a small survey. Ask five people one thing they liked and one thing they disliked about each candidate. Do not disregard personal statements made about a candidate. For example, Ms. Jones may have really liked the way in which a candidate dressed but did not like his position on aid to the elderly. You may discover that sometimes a person's vote is determined by a candidate's appearance, not by the candidate's platform. Record your findings in the diagram below. Then make a larger version of the diagram to present to the class.

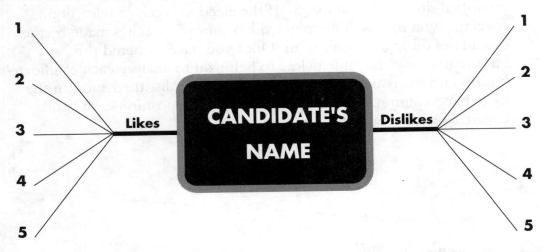

Next, research the election's outcome. Find out the percentage of votes each candidate received. Show this information in the form of a pie chart, similar to the following one.

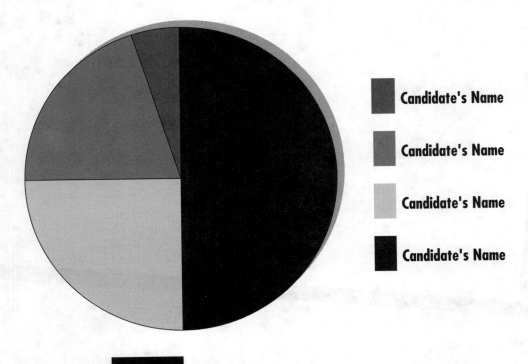

STEP 4

Presenting Your Findings..............

Finally, make a presentation to the class on the election that your group researched. Use charts and graphs to help your classmates better understand the candidates, the issues, and the election results.

Now that your group has finished its study on a local or state election, conclude the project by drawing conclusions. Answer the following questions as a group.

1. What part of the project did we find the most interesting to complete?

_____

_____

2. How helpful were the charts and graphs in summarizing the information about the election? _____

_____

3. How will this project help us to become more informed voters in future elections?

_____

_____

Evaluating Your Presentation.........

Evaluate your performance on this project by answering the following questions:

• Was our campaign information complete? What information was missing? Where might we have found this information?

• How would I rate my participation in group activities? Why?

• Were my group's charts and graphs helpful to the audience? Why or why not?

• Was my group's presentation effective? Why or why not?

• What grade would I give myself for this project? Why?

UNIT 2 TEST

1. State whether the following statement is true or false and explain your choice on the lines provided.

As a citizen in a democracy, you are required to vote in every national, state, and local election.

_____

_____

_____

Answer the following questions on the lines provided. Use examples and details to support your answers.

2. Why is it important to know both sides of an issue before casting a vote?

_____

_____

_____

_____

3. What are the limitations of getting your information about candidates or issues solely from what others tell you about them?

_____

_____

_____

_____

Answer the following essay question on a separate sheet of paper. Support your answer with examples and details.

4. Understanding community problems and their possible solutions is an important part of being an informed citizen. Imagine that you were just nominated to run for mayor of your city. Write an outline of your acceptance speech that reflects what you think are your community's most important issues and describes how you plan to deal with these issues.

UNIT 3

Using Your Freedoms of Expression

MANY

people think that the most important rights in a free society are the freedom of speech and the freedom of the press. Americans are very familiar and comfortable with these rights. In fact, they rarely give them a second thought. Every day, Americans freely express themselves in conversations, speeches, debates, concerts, and performances.

In this unit, you'll think critically about your freedoms of speech and press. You'll identify and interpret rights and responsibilities. You'll evaluate actions, draw conclusions, and express opinions. You'll examine the books that you read and the movies you see. You'll also discuss issues of censorship.

Free speech is a precious part of life in any community. As individuals, we learn and grow by listening to and reading about different experiences, ideas, and opinions. We can then use this information to form our own ideas and solve problems. For the unit project, you'll give a speech that offers a possible solution to a problem or that encourages a change.

Not in Our Community!

On his way home from school, Hector decided to take a detour. It was a clear spring day, and he had taken his camera with him. He wanted to take some pictures of his neighborhood in the spring. It was part of a special project that he was doing for his art class. He had taken photographs in the summer, fall, and winter, too. He thought the buildings were like people. They looked different in every season.

Hector aimed his camera at an empty store that used to sell groceries. *Snap!* Just two months ago, it had been full of life. Customers hurried in and out all day long. Now there was a big "For Rent" sign plastered across the store front. The paint was peeling and there were wooden boards covering the windows. He thought the building looked sad, like a person who had lost his way. *Snap!* He took one more picture before starting for home.

Hector was crossing Sixth Avenue when he noticed a truck pulling into the vacant lot on the corner. That's weird, he thought to himself. My dad said that no one has used the dump for a couple of years. Hector had taken pictures of the site last winter. It had been full of old tires and broken-down furniture. Sometimes homeless people slept there. In his photographs, the snow-covered objects looked like strange creatures from another world. He had even framed one of these

pictures and had hung it in his bedroom.

He checked his camera. There were six exposures left. *Snap!* He started shooting. Two men wearing white masks got out of the truck and threw some barrels into the rear of the lot. The place was so big that you couldn't see the barrels very clearly from the street. With so many boarded-up buildings, this part of town was usually deserted. Hector ran behind a parked car and crouched down as the truck pulled out of the lot. He waited until it turned at the corner. Then he walked around the lot to the far end. He took more pictures of the barrels. They had been piled on top of other barrels and metal containers. Some of them were rusted.

Hector noticed a thick liquid staining the ground around the containers. Then he noticed the smell. It was really awful. His nose and the inside of his mouth started to sting. He finished the roll of film and left quickly. He remembered the white masks that the two men were wearing. Now he understood why they didn't want to breathe the air around the dump. He didn't know what was in those barrels and containers. But from the smell, he guessed it was some sort of chemical. Whatever it was, it didn't belong in his community.

That night, Hector looked at his contact sheets, which showed each print on a roll of film. He used a magnifying glass to examine every picture. He was working so intently that he didn't hear the knock on his bedroom door.

"Hector," called his mother. "May I come in?"

"Sure, Mom," he answered. "Door's open."

He knew his mother was going to ask him about his English test. But this was so much more exciting than studying. He really was on to something.

"Look at this, Mom." He was pointing to

three different pictures on the contact sheets. "I took some photographs of that empty lot near Sixth Avenue. This one was taken last summer. These two were taken in the fall and winter." He handed the magnifying glass to his mother so that she could look at each tiny picture. "In the summer, the place was still empty, except for the old tires. But look at this. It was taken last fall. See those barrels?" Hector was pointing to one of the frames on a contact sheet. "I didn't think about it at the time. But today I took some more pictures. Two men were dumping more barrels in the lot this afternoon."

"Do you have any idea what could be inside?" his mother asked.

"It smelled like some kind of chemical. I think they're using the lot as an illegal dump. But I don't know what I can do about it."

"Why don't you start by developing all these pictures? Then develop the ones you took today. Let me see them when you've finished."

"Great," said Hector. "It shouldn't take too long."

"Just one thing," his mother said with a smile. "Don't forget to study for that English test."

"But, Mom," Hector said, "developing these prints is important." He couldn't believe that chemicals were being dumped right in their backyard. Well, almost in their backyard. He was collecting the proof. And what did his mother want him to do? Study for an English test.

"I agree with you, Hector. If you are right and chemicals are being dumped in that lot, it is important. And you have every right to do something about it. But it's going to take time, organization, and a lot of effort. So be prepared for a tough fight." Hector didn't realize it at the time, but his mother was right.

For the next two weeks, he continued to take pictures of the lot. The pile of barrels was growing. In one photograph, the barrels were resting against a chain-link fence, right under a sign that said, "No Dumping." Then he made enlargements of some of the photographs so that it was easier to see the barrels in the vacant lot.

He brought in his photographs to his social studies teacher, Mr. DePaul. The kids in the class looked at them. They had studied how toxic chemicals can affect the environment, polluting the water, air, and soil. As part of their project, they had talked to health department officials and the regional office of the Environmental Protection Agency. But none of the students had been aware of any toxic dumping in their community. Mr. DePaul looked at his students.

"Well," he said. "It's one thing to study about environmental pollution. It's something else to come face to face with it in our neighborhood. What do you think we should do now?"

Leroy raised his hand. "We come up with a plan to get the proof we need. I mean, we have to do something to stop this."

"Wait a minute," said Maria. "We already have the proof we need, right? Can't we go to the police or something?"

Mr. DePaul pointed to Hector's photographs. "Not until we know for certain what's inside those barrels. I think the best place to start would be the city health department. We can also find out if there's an emergency waste cleanup team in our city."

The students went to work right away. Hector and Maria wrote a letter to the city health department. Leroy and two other students contacted the regional office of the Environmental Protection Agency. They sent a letter outlining their suspicions, along with copies of Hector's photographs. The class waited expectantly. But there was no answer to their letter from the Environmental Protection Agency. Several more weeks passed.

"They're probably ignoring us," Maria said. "I guess they figure that a bunch of kids with some photographs aren't important enough to worry about."

But Hector wasn't so sure. One afternoon, he saw a van parked in front of the lot. He took a picture to show to the class. The words Environmental Protection Agency were on the side of the van. A week later, Mr. DePaul read a letter to the class. Researchers from the agency had checked out the lot. Their tests proved that Hector was right. Chemicals were being dumped in the lot illegally. All the students cheered when they heard the news.

Hector reported that he hadn't seen any new barrels left at the lot. He hoped that whoever was dumping the chemicals had been scared away.

"But that doesn't mean they're not going somewhere else," Lee Chin said.

"What about the barrels that are still there? Some of them are probably leaking. Who's going to clean that up?" Maria asked. "We have to let people know how we feel and what we have found out."

That night, Hector looked over his photographs again. They told a horrible story, and he wanted the people with the power to stop the illegal dumping to know the story. Mr. DePaul had told him that the city council was going to meet in just two weeks.

"Hector," Mr. DePaul said, "why don't you speak to the city council and tell the members what you know about the barrels in the dump site?"

"Do you think they'd pay attention to me?" Hector asked. "Maybe you or someone from the city health department would be better."

Mr. DePaul shook his head. "I don't think so, Hector. You have an important right. It's called *freedom of speech*. Don't ever be afraid to use it."

Hector thought about what Mr. DePaul said. Public speaking scared him, but this was important. He knew he had to do it. At first, his palms started to sweat whenever he practiced his speech. But he remembered his father's advice to keep it short and simple. "Tell them what you know and how you feel," his dad said. "They'll believe you and your pictures."

Two weeks later, Hector was ready. He walked into the city council meeting with copies of his photographs mounted on cardboard. I'll never get through this, he thought to himself. He walked slowly to the microphone and looked directly at his audience. In the back row, he saw the other kids from his class, his parents, and Mr. DePaul. Hector smiled at them and took a deep breath. "My name is Hector Morales. There's a serious problem in our city and I want to tell you about it . . ."

Lesson 1:
Interpreting the Message

Just what does the phrase *freedom of speech* mean? Is it your right to speak out and express your views and opinions, even if they disagree with the majority opinion? Is it your right to say anything you want, to anyone, anywhere, and at any time? Think about and respond to the following questions. Explain your answers.

1. Does a person have the right to give a speech about whether the mayor is doing a good job? _____

_____

_____

2. Does a person have the right to stand in the middle of an intersection at rush hour and give that speech? _____

_____

_____

3. Does a person have the right to try to persuade you to buy a particular tennis racket? _____

_____

_____

4. Does a person have the right to come into your classroom and try to persuade you and your classmates to buy that tennis racket?

_____

_____

5. Now look back over your answers. What can you say about the responsibilities that go along with freedom of speech? _____

_____

_____

Interpreting means to make an assessment or to give one's point of view. Interpretations are not facts. They are an expression of one's judgment or opinion, based on personal understanding and experience. For example, one person may interpret a waving arm as a greeting, while another might interpret this action as a warning. All learning requires interpretation, since we always bring our own thinking and experience to whatever we learn.

Freedom of the press for high school publications is a subject that is often debated. Some people think that students need guidance when expressing themselves in student newspapers and magazines. It is often the responsibility of a faculty adviser to

FREEDOM OF WHOSE SPEECH?

Sometimes people are better at respecting an idea than they are at respecting an idea in action. Consider the following question.

Is freedom of speech OK as long as someone doesn't disagree with you, have a different opinion, or offend you?

When you deal with issues of free speech for yourself and for others around you, it is important to remember that there is no free speech for *anyone* unless there is free speech for *everyone*.

Evaluation

Use the following questions to help you evaluate your performance on this lesson.

❏ Was I a good listener? If so, why? If not, what could I do to become a better listener?

❏ Was it difficult to listen respectfully to opinions that I disagreed with? If so, how did I handle this situation?

❏ Was I able to state clearly my opinions? How could I state them more clearly?

review all material submitted for publication and to censor it, if necessary. Other people think that students should be able to publish their newspapers and magazines without any form of censorship. What do you think? Should school publications be a place for students to express themselves without review or censorship? What should the role of a faculty adviser be?

Speak out about this issue. Outline your opinion and ideas below. Be sure to use examples to support your opinion.

_____

_____

_____

_____

_____

_____

_____

_____

_____

DISCUSSION

Dear Samantha,

I walk home every day after school. There's this kid in my class who lives in my neighborhood. He's really a jerk. He follows me home and calls me names. He makes fun of me and criticizes the way I look or dress. Sometimes he says he will do mean things, and he chases me. I tell him to stop it but he says, "I didn't do nothing to you. It's a free country, isn't it? I can say what I want." What should I do?

Signed,
Help

What do you think? Is it a "free country"? Can this person say whatever he wants to say? What should "Help" do? Talk about all of the options and decide on a course of action.

Lesson 2:
Arguing Your Case

Along with freedoms of expression comes an issue called *prior restraint*. **Prior restraint** refers to censorship. It refers to a process in which all printed materials are reviewed by someone in authority before the materials are published. This person could decide that an entire work, or parts of it, should not be printed.

The courts, especially the Supreme Court, protect Americans from this kind of system. Books, newspapers, and magazines are published without prior restraint. Speeches and lectures are given freely. Speakers do not need to worry about prior restraint by the government.

But what about censorship by others? Newspapers and magazines often include reports of people trying to ban, or remove, books from libraries and schools. Sometimes these people have been successful. Their argument is that some books are not suitable for children or young adults to read because the books are offensive or inappropriate in some way. Perhaps the books contain adult subject matter, controversial ideas, racial slurs, or obscene language. They may also encourage unacceptable or illegal behavior.

Think about the books that you have read recently. List them in the chart below. Be sure to include textbooks in your list.

Check the Yes column if you think that someone might object to something in the book. Then briefly describe the objection.

Caution!

The American Library Association printed the following list of books that some people consider to be offensive. You may see many books that you have read. Do you agree that these books should be banned? Why or why not?

A Separate Peace

A Wrinkle in Time

Alice's Adventures in Wonderland

Are You There, God? It's Me, Margaret

Catcher in the Rye

Cujo

Fallen Angels

Flowers for Algernon

Lord of the Flies

Our Bodies, Ourselves

Rosemary's Baby

Slaughterhouse-Five

The Adventures of Huckleberry Finn

The Chocolate War

The Exorcist

The Pigman

To Kill a Mockingbird

TITLE	YES	OBJECTION

THE LANGUAGE OF THINKING

Arguing means giving reasons for or against an issue or a proposal. When making an argument for or against something, it is important to support your opinion with details and examples. It is also important to use reason rather than emotion when presenting your views. Arguing different points of view should be done in the spirit of a challenge, with mutual respect and good will.

Get into small groups of three to four classmates. Discuss the novels that you have read recently. Consider which novels might be considered controversial. Choose one that everyone has read or a story with which everyone is familiar.

Then use the cluster map below to list subjects, characters, events, or other elements that some people might consider offensive or dangerous. Be sure to use specific details to support each element that you list.

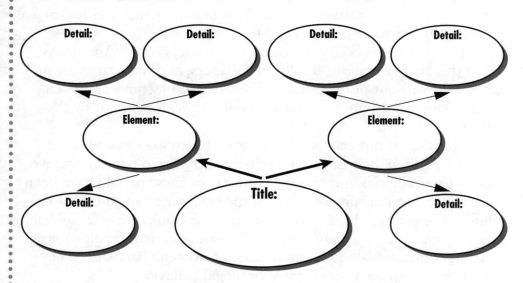

Stage a mock trial of the book in front of the class. Half of your group should argue in favor of banning your group's book in school, while the other half should argue against the ban. Members of the class will serve as your jury.

Before your trial begins, write below whether you will argue for or against banning the book. Then summarize the points you want to make during the trial. Remember to use specific examples and details. Regardless of whether you are pro or con, remember that your job is to persuade or convince the jury of your argument.

_____

_____

_____

_____

_____

_____

Lesson 3:
Assessing Issues and Answers

Questions about the freedoms of speech and press are always being asked. The answers are always controversial. Many of these controversies frequently seem removed from us and our personal experience, perhaps because they often involve politics and laws.

What about questions and controversies that touch your life? What about the books you read, the stories you write, the music you listen to, and the movies you see?

Think, for example, about the movie rating system, which was created by the movie industry itself. The purpose of the rating system is to identify the intended audience for a movie. The ratings also provide a warning to parents so that they can make decisions about the movies their children see.

Read the information in the sidenotes on this page and on page 42. Then fill out the questionnaire below.

QUESTIONNAIRE

1. Do you think that a rating system is needed? Why or why not?

_____

_____

_____

2. Do you pay attention to a movie's rating? Why or why not?

_____

_____

3. Do all of the "good" movies have one particular rating? If so, why?

_____

_____

_____

4. Should ratings reflect the quality of a movie? Why or why not?

_____

_____

_____

THE LANGUAGE OF THINKING

To **assess** something means to estimate or judge its value or worth. Making an assessment is the same as making an evaluation. An assessment, or evaluation, requires careful thinking. It requires that facts and information be combined with personal experiences and an understanding of the issue. An assessment is not a fact; it is a judgment. Two people, therefore, might make different assessments of the same thing.

MOVIE FACTS

❑ The current rating system for movies was 25 years old in 1993.

❑ 76 percent of parents with young children find the movie rating system effective and useful.

❑ 431 movies were released in 1992. Of the top 36 most successful movies that year, 18 were rated R, 7 were rated PG-13, 9 were rated PG, and 2 were rated G.

MOVIE RATINGS

The movie ratings below reflect the suitability of theme and content for people of different ages. These ratings are based on the degree to which a film contains questionable language, violence, sex, and drugs.

G = General Audiences (All ages admitted.)

PG = Parental Guidance Suggested (Some material may not be suitable for children.)

PG-13 = Parents Strongly Cautioned (Some material may be inappropriate for children under 13.)

R = Restricted (Children under 17 must be accompanied by a parent or an adult guardian.)

NC-17 = No children under 17 admitted

5. Should filmmakers be able to make movies about any subject they choose? _____
_____
_____

6. Why do you think that a majority of the most successful movies have PG-13 or R ratings? _____
_____
_____

7. Who really decides which movies people see? Explain your answer.
_____
_____
_____

What movies have you seen recently? List them in the chart below. Using the official rating system, give each film a rating of your own. Then check a newspaper or movie guide to fill in the official rating of the movie.

NAME OF MOVIE	MY RATING	OFFICIAL RATING

Compare the ratings in both columns. Talk about the possible reasons for the similarities or differences in the ratings.

Now go back and star the movies that you would recommend for a second grader. How do these movies compare with the ratings in the chart? What conclusions can you draw about your comparisons?
_____
_____
_____

Think about the music that teens listen to and the television programs that they watch. There are questions and controversies surrounding both of these areas. For example, many adults and teens attribute the increase of violence in public schools to the violent themes in movies and music.

Some people have proposed a rating system for music. The music would be rated for such things as obscene language and messages of hate and violence. Think about and respond to the questions below.

1. How would you assess this proposal? _____

_____

_____

2. Do you think singers and songwriters should be able to say whatever they like in their music? Why or why not? _____

_____

_____

3. Should television programs and music videos have a rating system? Explain your answer. _____

_____

_____

DISCUSSION

Rap music has often been under fire for many reasons. One reason has to do with a song called "Cop Killer," by Ice-T. In 1992, a police organization in Texas threatened to boycott the record's distributor, Time Warner. To many people, *rap* soon became a word that meant "scary, threatening, and violent."

Some people claim that this song and others like it are directly responsible for acts of violence in our cities and on our streets. Other people claim that this song is simply about the hard truths of life for some Americans. Ice-T himself said that "Cop Killer" is about an out-of-control, "psychopathic" character.

What do you think? Whose interpretation is correct? Is the word *rap* being fairly defined? Can song lyrics cause people to become violent?

BOOKSHELF

You can find many resources in a library or bookstore about freedom of expression. The following are just a few of the publications that are available. Check with your teacher, librarian, or a local bookstore owner for more titles.

Freedom of Expression: The Right to Speak Out in America, by Elaine Pascoe.

New Youth Connections. A national newspaper written and edited by teens.

Evaluation

Use the following questions to help you evaluate your performance on this lesson.

❑ Was it difficult to think objectively about movies I see or music I listen to? If so, why?

❑ Was it more difficult to respect other opinions about the movies and music I like? If so, how did I handle it?

❑ Did I change any of my opinions about the rights of others during this lesson? If so, what changed?

Speaking Out for Change

"There's always room for improvement!" is a slogan that is familiar to students everywhere. It is also a good slogan for many schools, neighborhoods, and communities. They, too, often have problems that need solving.

In Lesson 1, you read the stories of some people who exercised their freedom of speech, and you formed opinions about them. You then formed an opinion about censorship of student publications in schools and spoke out about it.

In Lesson 2, you learned about efforts by some people to ban books in schools and libraries. You then argued a case about banning a book in a mock trial. In Lesson 3, you examined questions and controversies about freedom of expression in movies and music lyrics. You also assessed the purpose and effectiveness of movie ratings.

People with ideas can change things and improve our lives. Some problems that we face in our communities are big ones, such as finding enough money to clean up environmental problems. Some problems are small ones, such as providing street-crossing guards for an elementary school or resolving conflicts in the schoolyard.

For this project, you will identify problems that people face or improvements that can be made in your school or community. After selecting one and forming an opinion about it, you will write and deliver a short speech that offers a solution to the problem or that encourages a change.

STEP 1 _Brainstorming and Choosing a Topic_..........................

With other members of a small group, take time to think about issues or problems that exist in your school or community. Brainstorm ideas. You might want to work in pairs within your group to generate a variety of topics.

Think about real examples and experiences in your life at home and in school. For example, one topic might be recycling. Is recycling something that could be improved upon in your home, school, or community? What kinds of things are recycled now? Could more be done? If so, how? As a group, answer the questions about recycling in the cluster map below. Then use the map to record other ideas. Review all of the ideas, then think again and add some more.

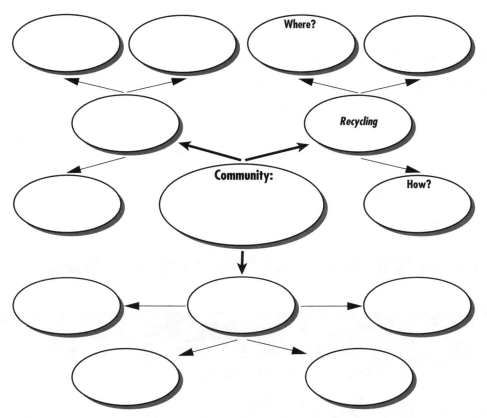

Now study the map of ideas that your group has assembled. Choose a topic that you would like to speak out about. Choose one that means something to you. Perhaps you know a lot about one of the topics, or you feel strongly about it. Or maybe you have had some personal experience with one of them.

STEP 2   Planning Your Speech.........

Decide what the purpose of your speech will be. Will you be speaking to inform your audience about a topic? Or will you be persuading people to accept your opinion or to do something? Or do you simply want to express an idea? What kind of solution or change will you propose?

Once you have decided on the purpose of your speech, make an outline of what you want to say. Decide whether you want to organize your material chronologically or whether you want to make your points one by one. Use the chart below to list information and to organize your thoughts. Use another sheet of paper, if necessary.

Topic:
....

Audience:
....

Purpose:
....

Solution or Change:
....

Outline

STEP 3

Writing the Speech...........................

Use your outline to write a draft of your speech. If sequence is important to the presentation of your topic, remember to use time-order words, such as first, next, after, then, and finally. If the purpose of your speech is to express an opinion, use language that will support that opinion. If you want to persuade your audience, use language that is persuasive and that encourages people to support you.

Exchange what you have written with a partner. Read over each other's work to suggest improvements. As you read, think about the topic. You might ask questions like the following:

• Is the topic clearly stated?

• Does the writer stick to the topic?

• Are ideas and opinions clearly expressed? Are they supported by reasons and examples?

- Do I understand what the writer is saying?
- Is the solution or suggestion for improvement realistic?

Practicing and Revising...............

Practice your speech out loud to someone. Decide whether there are any changes that you would like to make in what you said or in how you said it. Would gestures or props make your speech more effective? Is the speech too long? Is it too short? Be sure to practice your speech after each revision.

Presenting Your Speech....

Give your speech before the class. A successful speech depends on your preparation and confidence. Remember to stand tall, speak clearly, and look at your audience, or at some point behind the audience.

Evaluating Each Other's Speeches....

The success of a speech also depends on each listener. Listen carefully and evaluate what each person is saying and how it is being said. Evaluate each speaker, using the following questions:

- Was the speaker confident?
- If the speaker was giving information, was the information complete?
- If the speaker was trying to persuade, was the argument convincing?
- If the speaker was expressing an opinion, was the opinion supported by reasons and examples?

*U*sing the answers to these questions, evaluate the effectiveness of each speech by rating it from 1 to 5. If the speech was very poorly planned and presented, give it

UNIT 3 TEST

1. Tell whether this statements is true or false. Explain your answers on the lines provided.

Freedom of speech means that people can say anything they want at any time and in any place.

_____

_____

_____

Answer the following questions on the lines provided. Use examples and details to support your answers.

2. How does using reason, rather than emotion, change the way you prepare to argue a point?

_____

_____

_____

3. In Lesson 3, you learned about the rating system that the movie industry has developed for films that are shown in the United States. Some people think that this system is effective. Others think that it is unnecessary. With which opinion do you agree? Give reasons to support your opinion.

_____

_____

_____

? **Answer the following essay question on a separate sheet of paper. Support your answer with examples and details.**

4. People who argue for issues of free speech and a free press often point out that there is no freedom of expression for anyone if we do not guarantee these freedoms to everyone. What do they mean? Are these freedoms alive in your school or community today? What can you do to protect these freedoms in your community or school?

48

UNIT 4

Advertising: The Persuasion Game

You are exposed to advertisements every day. You see advertisements while you watch television, listen to the radio, read magazines and newspapers, and walk around your community. Advertisements have even entered the home video and computer markets. An advertisement is any paid message that calls attention to a product, service, or idea. It can include radio and television commercials, billboards, store windows, business cards, and so on.

In this unit, you'll think critically about several advertising issues. You'll observe and research the many sources of advertisements. In addition, you'll conduct an analysis of a target audience. You'll predict what teens will be like in the future and how advertisers might tap into this new teen market. You'll also examine and debate advertising censorship issues.

As technology advances, our concept of community expands. Technology brings people all across the world together. Businesses can now more easily sell products in other countries. As a unit project, you'll create an advertisement to sell a U.S. product to teens in another country.

Advertising Questionaire

How well do you pay attention to the commercials on TV or to the advertisements in the magazines and newspapers that you read? To test your advertising knowledge, fill in the following questionnaire. Then compare your responses with those of your classmates.

1. Describe the commercial or advertisement that you think of first when you read or hear each of the following words or phrases. Explain why that commercial or advertisement is memorable.

a. athletic shoes _____

_____

_____

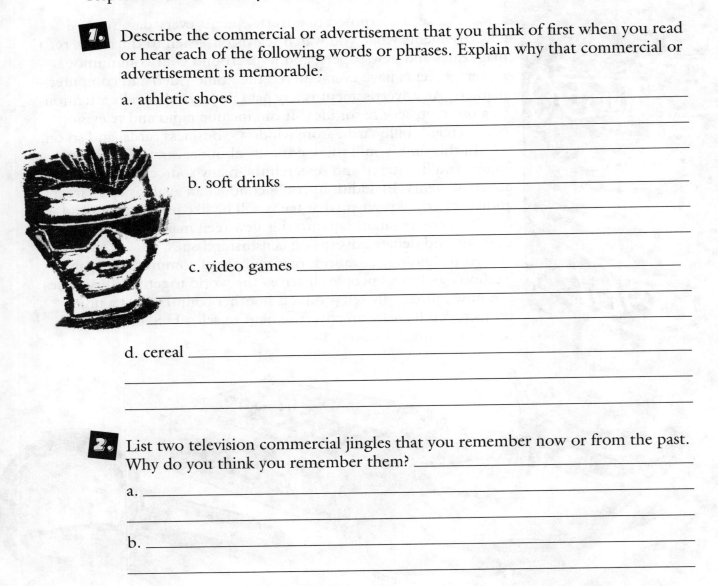

b. soft drinks _____

_____

_____

c. video games _____

_____

_____

d. cereal _____

_____

_____

2. List two television commercial jingles that you remember now or from the past. Why do you think you remember them? _____

a. _____

_____

b. _____

_____

3. What is your favorite television commercial? Why? _____
_____
_____

4. What is your least favorite television commercial? Why? _____
_____
_____
_____

5. What ads or commercials have you seen today? List the product or the
company's name for every ad you recall seeing. _____
_____
_____
_____

6. Do you pay attention to advertisements in the magazines and newspapers that
you read? Why or why not? _____
_____
_____
_____

7. What products have you purchased as a result of an advertisement you saw or read?
_____
_____
_____

8. Do you think advertisements influence what you buy? Explain. _____
_____
_____

As technology continues to advance, advertisers are discovering new high-tech sources for advertising. Here are just a few:

Video Kiosks. Manufacturers have set up videotape monitors in department stores that continuously run ad presentations.

Computer Networks. Home computers linked to computer networks can receive ads.

Home Shopping Channels. Department stores may lead the way in setting up their own cable network home shopping channels. Others have already taken advantage of the popular QVC channel.

CD-ROM. Many advertisers are looking at ways to enter the CD-ROM market as periodicals become computerized.

Lesson 1:
Categorizing Ads and Commercials

Advertising is all around us. We have become so used to seeing advertising that we aren't even aware of its influence. Studies show that Americans receive approximately 1,600 advertising messages a day! That's an astounding number, considering how unaware of them we have become.

Today, you are going to record as many sources of advertising that you can think of and observe in your community. Using the chart below, list under each category the places where we find advertising messages. If you think of more categories, be sure to add them to the chart.

SOURCES OF ADVERTISING

Magazines Newspapers	Television Radio	Other Technology
Signs	Product Packaging	Mailers
Unusual Sources	Other	

On your way home from school today, look for other places and ways in which people advertise goods and services in your community. Add them to your chart.

Referring to the sources you wrote in the chart, answer the following questions.

1. Which source of advertising are you most likely to notice? Why?

_____

_____

2. Does the source of the advertisement affect how it influences

you? Why or why not? _____

_____

_____

Technology is a new source that advertisers are just beginning to explore and use. Read the sidenote on page 52 about high-tech advertising that is already taking place.

3. How might technology, such as interactive computers and

virtual reality, influence advertising? _____

_____

_____

4. How effective do you think those sources of advertising will be?

Explain. _____

_____

_____

DISCUSSION

In 1993, a private company called Space Marketing Concepts, Inc., proposed before Congress to launch a billboard into space. The mile-long billboard would be seen by the entire Western Hemisphere. It would burn out about 10 to 14 days later. The Georgia-based company said that the billboard would advertise the sponsor's environmental products. The proposal nevertheless received strong negative reaction, especially from astronomers and environmentalists. Congress did not pass the proposal. Do you think Congress was right in not passing the proposal? Why or why not? Should outer space become a giant billboard?

Evaluation

Use the following questions to help you evaluate your performance on this lesson.

❑ Did I find at least 15 different sources of advertising?

❑ Do I consider myself a keen observer? Why or why not?

❑ What are the sources of advertising that I didn't know before?

❑ What did I discover about the influence of advertising?

Lesson 2:
Analyzing Target Audiences

TARGET AUDIENCE

A target audience is the audience that a business most wants to reach. Advertisers divide markets into categories, including age, sex, income level, education, geographic region, ethnic background, political affiliation, lifestyle, and so on.

PERSUASION TECHNIQUES

Testimonials use celebrities or authority figures as spokespeople to endorse a product. Which celebrities endorse soft drink companies? athletic shoes?

Testimonials can also use **scientific or statistical data** to convince audiences that one product is the best: for example, "Four out of five doctors use Brand X vitamins." These advertisements frequently do not name the source of the data.

Bandwagon refers to an advertisement that shows a large group of people using a product. The advertisement invites the audience to become part of the group.

Advertisers carefully consider who their audience is or who they want their audience to be. They call this the **target audience**. Once they define their target audience, advertisers buy commercial spots at times when that audience is most likely to be watching television. Compare the types of products advertised on Saturday morning with those advertised at night or during the weekday. To whom are advertisers appealing in each time slot? Similarly, magazine advertisers buy space in magazines that appeal to their target audience's interests.

Select one print advertisement from a magazine or newspaper you currently read. Who is the target audience? As you answer the following questions, think of yourself as a member of the target audience.

1. What are the characteristics and interests of the target audience?

_____

_____

2. Do you have the characteristics and interests of the target audience? Explain. _____

_____

_____

3. How does this advertisement grab your attention? _____

_____

_____

_____

4. What technique(s) does the advertisement use to try to persuade you to like or buy the product? Read about several persuasive techniques that advertisers use in the sidenotes on pages 54 and 55. _____

_____

_____

_____

5. Would you buy or use this product? Why or why not? _____
_____
_____

6. How would you improve the advertisement so that it is more appealing to you? _____
_____
_____

PUBLIC-SERVICE CAMPAIGNS

Public-service campaigns are becoming more common on television. These commercials do not sell products. They primarily make audiences aware of health and safety risks. Who are the target audiences for these commercials? In the chart below, record two public-service campaigns that you have seen on television. Describe the campaign, the interests or values it appeals to, the message it conveys, and the target audience.

Public Service Commercial	Appeals To	Message	Target Audience

7. Are you among the target audience for one or both of these campaigns? Explain. _____
_____

8. Are these commercials effective? Why or why not? _____
_____
_____
_____

• • • • • • • • • • •
MORE PERSUASION TECHNIQUES

Card stacking refers to several techniques in which advertisers only give half truths.

❑ An **unfinished claim** states that one product is better but doesn't finish the comparison: for example, "Brand X gives you more." More than what?

❑ The **"we're different and unique" claim** emphasizes that a product is special or unique.

❑ The **"water is wet" claim** states something about a product that is true for any brand of the same product.

Evaluation
• • • • • • • • •

Use the following questions to help you evaluate your performance on this lesson.

❑ What did I learn about target audiences and advertising techniques?

❑ What did I find difficult about analyzing an audience? Why?

❑ How might I apply what I learned about advertising to my daily life?

Lesson 3:
Predicting Teen Audiences in 2010

TEEN CONSUMERS

According to Nickelodeon, in 1992, the average weekly income of teenagers between 14 and 17 was approximately $34.

TEEN SPEAK

To sell to the teen market, advertisers should just speak to teens in their language. Right? Wrong. According to many advertising agencies, advertisers should not use slang. By the time adults who write the advertisements are aware of the latest expressions, the slang is too popular to be "hip"—or whatever the current slang expression is. In addition, the life of slang is just too short to be an effective advertising tool.

Teens in the United States make up a major group of consumers. Studies show that teens spend about $56 billion a year on products. But are advertisers hitting the mark as far as teens are concerned? Which advertisements really influence the teen market?

As we approach the twenty-first century, advertisers will have to predict what teens of the new century will be like. Imagine that you are a teen consultant for a major advertising agency. You must advise the advertising executives about what teens in the year 2010 will be like.

1. First, think about what today's teens are like and fill in the chart below. Then jot down your ideas about what teens in 2010 might be like.

Teens Today	Teens in 2010
Interests: *music* *clothes*	**Interests:**
Concerns: *environment* *economy*	**Concerns:**

2. Using your notes from the chart, write a memo to the advertising agency. In the memo, describe what you think teens will be like in the next century. Tell the agency what teens might be interested in. Also tell what teens might be doing and what their communities might be like.

To:

From:

Date:

Re: Advertising to Teens in 2010

3. How might advertisers best reach teens of the twenty-first century? _____
_____
_____
_____

4. What media might advertisers of the twenty-first century most effectively use? Why? _____
_____
_____
_____

BOOKSHELF

You can find many resources in a library or bookstore about advertising and censorship. The following are just a few of the books and magazines that are available. Check with your teacher, librarian, or a local bookstore owner for more titles.

Caution! This May Be an Advertisement: A Teen Guide to Advertising, by Kathlyn Gay.

The School on Madison Avenue: Advertising and What It Teaches, by Ann E. Weiss.

Advertising, by Richard O. Pompian.

Evaluation

Use the following questions to help you evaluate your performance on this lesson.

❏ What did I find difficult about predicting what teens will be like in the future? How did I overcome these difficulties?

❏ Would the memo I wrote be helpful to an advertising agency? Why or why not?

Lesson 4:
Debating Issues of Censorship

TV CENSORSHIP

Does advertising control the content of television shows? Or do TV networks censor the ads it will run? Actually, both are true.

Television advertisers will pull out if they do not like a program's content. The pressure is often so great that networks will cancel a show, move the show to a different time slot, or change the show to meet advertisers' approval.

On the other hand, television networks determine which ads they will run. For example, they won't broadcast commercials that make fun of television. They will also often censor ads that take controversial positions on important topics.

Censorship is the act of removing or changing anything thought not right or appropriate for people to see, hear, or read. For example, books, magazines, and music have been censored from schools, libraries, and stores. Products have also been banned. For example, there was a time when cigarette commercials were broadcast on television. But in 1971, Congress passed a bill banning, or censoring, cigarette commercials from television. Many people believed that these commercials were encouraging young people to start smoking.

Some people now believe that beer commercials are as harmful as cigarette commercials. Nevertheless, beer commercials continue to appear on television. What do you think? Should Congress also ban beer commercials? What have beer companies done to try to improve their images? Have their efforts to improve these images been successful?

Form two groups. Those who think beer commercials are a bad influence on young people should form one group. Those who think that they are not a bad influence should form another group. In your group, list either the pros or the cons of keeping beer commercials on television. Do not limit your argument only to voicing your personal opinions. Research the controversy so that you can include facts and examples to support your statements. Use the graphic organizer below to list the points that you want to debate.

DEBATING TIP

While the other team presents its position, take careful notes. Jot down the points the speaker makes. Then use your notes to remind yourself of the points you need to cover during the rebuttal.

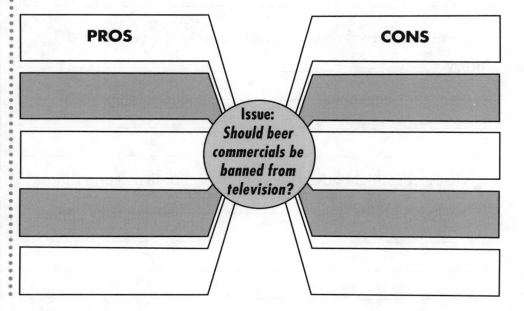

PROS   CONS

Issue:
Should beer commercials be banned from television?

58

Think about the following points as you form your group's position:

- Who is the target audience of beer commercials and advertisements?
- To what do the commercials and advertisements appeal?
- What persuasive technique(s) do they use?
- What hidden messages do they convey?
- What facts should you know about beer and alcohol?

Summarize the three most important points that support your group's position.

1. _____
_____
_____

2. _____
_____
_____

3. _____
_____
_____

As a class, debate this issue. Make sure that during the debate your group covers at least the three important points you identified above.

DISCUSSION

In addition to its ban from television, the tobacco industry is again under attack. This time people are attacking the "Joe Camel" advertisements in magazines and on billboards. Some people believe that Camel's mascot will attract young smokers. Does he attract a young audience? If yes, how does he attract them? Do you think "Joe Camel" should be banned? Why or why not?

What efforts has your school or local community taken to support or discourage the tobacco industry?

Selling to Teens: An International Outlook

Technology has expanded the concept of community. We now live in an international community. Technology allows us to communicate easily and quickly with other parts of the world. Businesses can now sell their products to entirely new audiences much more rapidly than before.

In Lesson 2, you learned that advertisers analyze their target audiences to find ways of grabbing the audience's attention or appealing to their interests. In Lesson 3, you predicted what teens in the twenty-first century will be like.

For this project, you are again being asked to act as a teen consultant for an advertising agency. You must find out what teens in another country are like and what American products they would be interested in buying. You'll research the culture of the country you choose. You'll then create an advertisement to sell a U.S. product to teens in that country.

STEP 1 Researching and Gathering Information.........................

In a small group, choose a country you would like to research. Use the web below to brainstorm possible research subtopics. For example, one topic might be weather and climate. This information could be important to help you decide what products the teens in your chosen country would buy and use. If they live in a warm climate, you might not try to sell them ski equipment. You must also research what the country's youth is like. Think of other information that would be helpful in deciding what products to advertise. Add them to your web as well.

Decide as a group which member will be responsible for each of the topics you have identified. Use a variety of sources for your research, including encyclopedias, magazines, travel books, and nonfiction books about the country or people you are researching. Take careful notes so that you can present your information to the group.

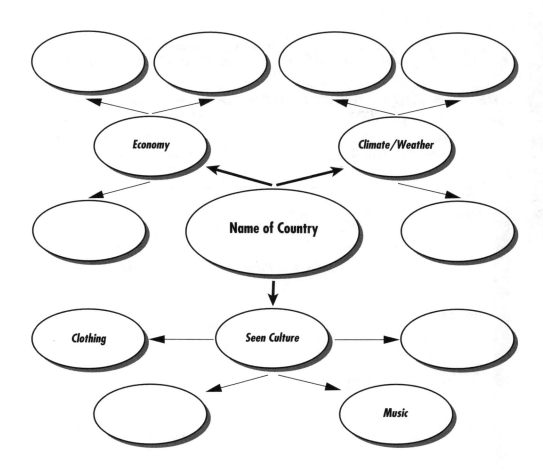

Presenting Information.........

Next, present your topics to the group. As each member is speaking, jot down key words, facts, or ideas about the country in the left column of the following chart. In the right column, list possible products that your target audience might use.

After filling in the chart, each group member should have a fairly good idea of the types of products that your target audience might be interested in. As a group, select the one item from your charts that everyone thinks has the best chance of being sold in the country you researched.

Key Words	Product Ideas

Analyzing a Product······

Just as they analyze audiences, advertising executives closely examine the products for which they are developing an advertisement. They list positive words, feelings, and ideas that come to mind as they look at and use the product. Use the following chart to help you analyze the strengths of your product.

Product Analysis of _____ *(name of product)*	
	Words and Phrases That Describe
Appearance	
Function	
Appeal	
Benefits	

STEP 4

Writing an Advertisement······

Working with your group, you will now use the chart above to create your product advertisement. For this project, you can create either a print or a video advertisement. Look again at several examples of print advertisements and television commercials. These examples will give you some ideas about how you might put together your advertisement. If you are creating a print advertisement, decide if you want a slogan or a product description or both. Think about what visual image, or picture, you want to show. For a video advertisement, decide if you want a jingle or music to accompany the visual images and the dialogue that you present.

*W*ith your group, develop an advertisement for your target audience. As you write the script or advertising copy, use some of the words and phrases that you listed in Step 3 that tell your audience what the benefits of the product are. Remember, your goal is to use words and images that will appeal to your target audience's interests and grab its attention. Keep in mind also the country in which your target audience lives.

Presenting Your Advertisement.......

Present your advertisement to the class in an oral presentation. Ask the class to identify possible target audiences. Have one member of your group record the responses. As classmates call out possible target audiences, ask them to give reasons for their responses. Then tell the class who the target audience is and explain why your group thinks your target audience will be interested in the product. In addition, tell why you believe your advertisement will grab your audience's attention or will persuade it to buy and use the product.

Evaluating..

The advertising industry presents Cleo awards to the creators of television commercials. Decide as a class which group deserves a Cleo for best or most creative commercial or advertisement. Cast your vote based on creativity, the advertisement's or commercial's ability to capture your interest, the quality of the presentation, and the appropriateness of the product for the target audience.

••

1. Circle the correct answer and explain your choice on the lines provided.
It is important to understand the techniques advertisers use to attract our
attention in order to be
a. an informed consumer.   c. a member of a target audience.
b. a victim of advertising.   d. an organized thinker.

_____

_____

2. Check the box of the true statement and explain your choice on the lines
provided.
❑ Good critical thinkers gather and organize information before making an
informed judgment.
❑ Good critical thinkers consider only their opinions before making an informed
judgment.

_____

_____

Answer the following question on the lines provided.

3. If a business really wanted to reach today's teens through advertising, who might
it hire to act as its spokesperson? Why would this person be effective?

_____

_____

_____

_____

? **Answer the following essay question on a separate sheet of paper. Support your
answer with examples and details.**

4. People often say that advertising presents a portrait of American society. In other
words, advertisements reflect the current interests and values of Americans in
general. Think about the advertisements that you observed in your community.
Describe what those advertisements tell about the interests and values of the
people in your community. Do you think they accurately reflect your community?
Why or why not?

64

UNIT 5

Consumerism: Buyers Beware!

A consumer is a person who buys something or uses a service of some kind. You are probably very familiar with buying things and using services. Think for a moment about the many different items that fill the grocery stores, specialty shops, and department stores in your community alone.

In addition to typical purchases of food and clothing, people buy such things as water, electricity, and gas for cooking and heating. People also need to purchase different kinds of services. Garbage removal, telephone installation, car and stereo repairs, haircuts, and medical and dental services are just a few examples.

Making decisions about how to spend money and what to buy are important issues for consumers. Becoming a good shopper means becoming a good decision maker. It means having the skills to choose quality products for fair prices. Becoming a good consumer takes time and thought.

In this unit, you'll inventory the purchases that you made in the past month and assess the choices that you made. You'll examine some advertising claims for products that you use regularly. You'll also identify what is factual and what is not factual in these claims. You'll take a critical look at the contents of an owner's manual and product warranty. Working with purchases from a typical month, you'll develop a budget for next month.

The number of products available to consumers today is always increasing. The choices can sometimes seem overwhelming. In this unit, you'll acquire shopping and money-management skills. For the unit project, you'll apply these skills as you make a decision about which portable radio-cassette player to buy.

65

LET THE BUYER THINK TWICE

For the first time in a long time, Leroy got up early on a Saturday morning. In fact, he actually was out of bed before his alarm went off. Leroy didn't usually set his alarm on weekends. But this wasn't an ordinary weekend. Tonight was the last basketball game of the season. The winning team would play in the citywide championship next month. This game was going to be incredible to watch. It was going to be even more incredible to play in. And Leroy was scheduled to start as the team's center.

He looked at his uniform. It was folded neatly on top of his desk. Actually, the uniform was probably the only neatly folded item of clothing in Leroy's room. But he wasn't thinking about that. He was concentrating on the blue-and-white T-shirt and the white shorts. He was studying the number on the back of his T-shirt. It was number 43—his number. Boy, he felt proud.

Then Leroy looked down at his high-tops. He had been wearing them all year to practice, and he hadn't realized how torn they were. The rubber was starting to peel away from the heel and toe of the right shoe. Even the sole on the left shoe looked pretty worn.

Automatically, Leroy looked back at his basketball uniform. He thought about all the baskets he would score in the game that night. He could see himself dribbling down the court, jumping, and shooting the ball. The basketball would soar through the air—swish! Two points. He could hear the crowd cheering. They would scream his name—Leroy, Leroy!

Of course, there was another possibility. While he was running down the court, he could fall flat on his face. It would happen because of his worn shoes. He could just imagine rubber soles giving way and tripping him face first.

Face it, Leroy said to himself. These are definitely not the shoes of a winner. Besides, all the other guys on the team had new shoes. At least, they looked new to Leroy. When he had mentioned this fact to his mother, she told him to have the rubber soles replaced. It would be a lot cheaper to repair the shoes than to buy new ones.

Leroy considered his mother's suggestion. Then he considered the money he had earned delivering papers last summer. He had saved most of it. He had even made up a budget so that he would spend his savings only on the things he really needed. That way, he would still have some money left at the end of the semester.

Leroy's budget did not include a new pair of high-tops. OK, he thought to himself, I'm going to follow Mom's advice. I'll go to the shoe-repair shop this morning, right after breakfast.

On his way downstairs, Leroy noticed a magazine he had been reading before going to bed. There was a full-page advertisement for high-tops staring him in the face. They weren't ordinary high-tops, either. Leroy's favorite basketball star was wearing them.

Leroy studied the picture in the advertisement. Of course, the advertisement didn't say that the shoes were responsible for the basketball player's amazing jumps. Still, Leroy thought, this guy is the very best. And he does wear these shoes in every game. Maybe it wouldn't be such a bad idea to look in a few stores before I go to the shoe-repair shop.

Leroy was still studying the advertisement while he finished his breakfast. Another magazine and two newspapers covered the breakfast table. Leroy's mother patted him on the arm approvingly when she entered the kitchen.

"Leroy," she said. "I'm so glad to see you keeping up with the news. It's important to know what's going on in the world."

Since his mouth was full of cereal, Leroy could only nod. Unfortunately, his mother decided to look more closely at the newspapers and magazines in front of him. A dozen different advertisements for high-tops stared back at her.

"Well," she sighed, "I knew it was too good to be true."

"Mom, I was just about to read that front-page story about the economy," Leroy said. "But I saw these ads, and I thought I would just take a look."

His mother tapped the magazine with her finger. "In other words, you're going to buy a new pair of high-tops, right?" she asked.

Leroy nodded. "I have to buy them before tonight's game."

"Well, it's your money. But I hope you compare prices—and quality, before making your choice," his mother said.

Leroy pointed to the magazine and newspaper advertisements. "That's part of the problem. All of them say the same things." He read from one of the advertisements, " 'An incredible buy. Lowest price in town. Best value.' " Then he put down the magazine and shrugged. "The high-tops all look alike, too. I don't know where to begin to look for a pair."

His mother sat down at the table with her cup of coffee. "Why don't you start with a store? Try on a couple of pairs of shoes and see how they feel on your feet. Remember, you're the one who's going to be wearing them, not the star in the ad. You know that wearing a new pair of shoes won't make you the star of the basketball team."

Leroy had to admit it, his mother did have a point. Still, the shoes really looked terrific—in all of the ads. And if he bought a pair, maybe he would jump a little higher. He might even make the game's winning basket.

OK, Leroy thought to himself, it's time for a little comparison shopping. I'll go to a couple of the shoe stores in the mall and check out the prices. I'll forget about these ads. They're too confusing anyway.

Leroy was about to throw away the magazine when something caught his eye. It was an advertisement for the same high-tops that his friend Alan had bought a few weeks ago. These shoes were on sale for two more days. If Leroy bought them, he would have money left over.

On the way to the mall, Leroy thought about the new CD he would be able to buy. He made a shopping plan in his head. After buying the new high-tops and the CD, he would check out the video store. Maybe he would even have money left over for a burger. He had reviewed his financial situation before leaving the house. There would definitely be enough money to pay for the new shoes and more. He felt terrific.

Leroy was still feeling great when he walked into the shoe store on the lower level. He looked around and realized that the store had nothing but high-tops. Everywhere he looked, there were dozens of different high-tops.

Leroy started to look for the brand he had seen advertised in the newspaper. Of course, he didn't think those would be the only shoes in the store. The problem was, he didn't realize just how many different kinds of high-tops there were.

There must be a million different brands, Leroy thought to himself. OK, not a million—but at least a hundred.

He remembered his shopping plan. He was going to look over all the styles and brands in his price range. But the more he looked, the harder it was to remember exactly what his price range was. Everything in the store started to look the same. And everything seemed too expensive for him.

Leroy was about to leave when he remembered his worn high-tops back in his room. He looked at his watch. It was too late for the shoe-repair store. His shoes would never be resoled in time for the game.

Leroy overheard another customer as she tried on a pair of shoes. She was talking about such things as arch support and cushioning. Leroy didn't even know what they meant. All he knew was that he needed a pair of high-tops and a burger, in that order.

A salesperson approached Leroy. "May I help you?" he asked.

Leroy pointed to the shoes in the advertisement. Then he pointed to his feet. "I'd like to buy these shoes in size . . ." But before he could finish, the salesperson shook his head. Suddenly, Leroy knew he was in trouble.

"Too bad you didn't get here just a little sooner," he said. "We're out of stock on those shoes. With a price like that, those high-tops just walked right out of here." The salesperson couldn't resist laughing at his own joke. Leroy could. Maybe he should have followed his mother's advice and had his old shoes repaired last week. Maybe he should just go home.

"I can see you're disappointed," the

salesperson said. "But we have another brand that's just as good as the one in the ad. Personally, I think these shoes are even better. They really cushion your feet. Let me get you a pair."

A few minutes later, Leroy was looking at himself in the long mirror. The high-tops he was trying on looked the same as the shoes in the ad. There was only one problem—the price.

"How do they feel?" the salesperson asked.

Leroy pointed to his big toe. "Actually, they're a little tight there."

"Don't worry," said the salesperson. "They'll adjust to your foot. You have to break them in. Why not walk around on the carpet a little?"

Leroy took a few steps. He had to admit, the shoes did feel more comfortable. He turned to the salesperson. "What did you say they were made out of?"

The salesperson was looking at a customer at the other end of the store. "It's a new lightweight fabric. All the better high-tops will be made with it this year. It gives you more bounce and lets your feet breathe when you walk."

Leroy tried to pretend he understood. "Is it important for your feet to breathe?"

The salesperson sounded a little impatient. "Very," he said. He looked at his watch. Then he started putting the other shoes back in their boxes.

Leroy felt a little nervous. He knew he should make up his mind soon.

"I don't want to pressure you," the salesperson said. "If you'd like to look around some more. We have a special on those shoes," he said, pointing to a rack behind Leroy.

Leroy had noticed the shoes when he first walked into the store. But the price tag on the shoes marked "Special" wasn't any lower than the price tag on some of the other shoes in the store. He looked down at the high-tops he was wearing. Then he looked back at the salesperson.

Less than five minutes later, Leroy was walking home from the mall, carrying two large shopping bags. One contained his new high-tops. The other contained a pair of sneakers he had bought at the last minute. The salesperson said that he would never find a pair like that at a cheaper price. What could Leroy do?

That night Leroy proudly laced up his new high-tops in the locker room before the game. He knew that his parents and brothers would be watching from the bleachers. He would score his first basket for them.

When Leroy and his teammates walked out onto the basketball court, the crowd went wild. Leroy's heart was pounding. With his new high-tops, he couldn't fail. Didn't the salesperson say the special fabric would give him more bounce?

The game started. Leroy forgot about his new shoes. He forgot about his family in the bleachers. Now the ball was his. He dribbled down the court. He jumped, aimed at the basket, but he didn't score.

Later that night while walking home from the game with his family, Leroy didn't say much. His father put his arm around Leroy's shoulder. "You did a good job out there tonight, son. We're all proud of you."

Leroy felt a little better. "Thanks, Dad. At least I made one basket. But I thought I could score a lot more points. I guess my new shoes weren't so special after all."

"Probably not," his father said. "But you are, with or without a new pair of shoes. If you have time tomorrow, maybe we can get in some practice. I just have to dig out my old pair of sneakers. To tell you the truth, I never went in for those fancy high-tops."

Leroy smiled at his father. "I feel the same way, Dad."

Lesson 1:
Making Choices

Have you ever walked into a store to buy a specific product but couldn't decide which one to buy because there were so many items from which to choose? Many people face this problem when they shop. They become confused by the many different brands and styles available. Often they buy things that they don't want or need. How do you make decisions when faced with so many choices?

Take a few minutes to think about what you actually bought during the past month. Then fill in the chart below. List each item under an appropriate category. For example, jeans and sweaters might be listed under "Clothing," and swimsuits and tennis balls might be listed under "Sporting Goods." Shampoo, deodorant, and cosmetics could be listed under "Personal Products." Compact discs and movie tickets could be listed under "Entertainment."

Clothing	Shoes	Personal Products	Sporting Goods

Entertainment	Food	Transportation	Hobbies

Look back over the items that you listed in your chart. Star those purchases that you consider to be "good" ones. Choose one of those purchases and explain why you gave it a star.

_____

_____

_____

Now review your list again. Think about the purchases that do not have stars. Circle the purchases with which you are unhappy for some reason. Choose one and explain why you're not satisfied with it.

_____

_____

_____

If you needed to buy one of the circled items again, what could you do to make a better choice? The information in the sidenotes on both pages of this lesson will give you some ideas.

_____

_____

_____

DISCUSSION

Some companies use labels on their boxes or containers that can be misleading. The labels "Economy Size" and "Family Size," for example, are often used to imply "more for less." In some cases, however, these sizes are not the most economical ones to buy.

Sometimes the packages themselves can be misleading. A cereal company, for example, has been hiding price increases by putting smaller amounts of cereal inside its boxes. To make matters worse, it uses a new image or color design on the box, labels it "new," and charges the same price or even more than for the old one!

What do you think about these practices? How can consumers complain about labeling and packaging practices they think are unfair? How can you, as a consumer, protect yourself against these practices?

● ● ● ● ● ● ● ● ● ● ● ●
SHOPPING DON'TS

❏ Don't buy an item just because it is on sale.

❏ Don't buy items from displays marked "Special" unless you have investigated the price first. "Special" displays do not always have the lowest prices.

❏ Don't be swayed because an item you haven't seen before is blocking your path down an aisle. Avoid impulse buying!

❏ Don't buy more than you need just because they're bargains.

❏ Don't shop for groceries on an empty stomach. All foods look good when you're hungry.

Evaluation

● ● ● ● ● ● ● ● ● ●

Use the following questions to help you evaluate your performance on this lesson.

❏ What did I learn that will make me a better decision maker and consumer?

❏ Was I generally pleased with my review of my past shopping decisions? Why or why not?

❏ What did I do well in this lesson?

THE LANGUAGE OF THINKING

A critical reader actively looks for key concepts, facts, opinions, and reasons while reading. A critical reader also interprets what is being read and checks for understanding.

• • • • • • • • • • • •

WHAT IS A FACT?

A fact is something that actually happened or is known to be true. A fact can be proved, or verified. A fact can be used to support an opinion, interpretation, or estimation.

❑ **Fact or Nonfact?**
This cereal is made of rice. (*Fact:* The main ingredient listed is rice.)

❑ **Fact or Nonfact?**
This cereal is the breakfast of superstars. (*Nonfact:* Which superstars? Who are they? What do they eat for breakfast? This statement implies that all people who eat this cereal are superstars. Do you think this claim is true?)

Lesson 2:
Reading Ads Critically

Being a smart shopper is often a matter of reading more than just advertising claims or the labels on a package. In advertisements and commercials, manufacturers almost always claim that their products are the best or at least better than the others. They may also claim that using their products will make you a better or more attractive person in some way. How can you tell whether these claims are true?

Consumer groups study and test products and their advertising claims. They then report their findings to the public. These reports are frequently published in newspapers and magazines. There are even television programs, called "infomercials," that test the claims of various products in front of studio audiences.

Do some testing of your own. Go through a newspaper or magazine and find some examples of advertisements for two or three products that you often buy or use, such as toothpaste or your favorite cereal or soft drink. If possible, cut out the advertisements that you select.

Read each advertisement carefully. Then fill out the chart below by identifying each product for which you have an advertisement. List the claims made by each advertisement.

Product	Claims
1.	
2.	
3.	

Using the claims you listed in the chart above, fill in the two columns below—with the facts and nonfacts in the claims.

FACTS	NONFACTS

Look back at the columns of facts and nonfacts. Which column has more listings? What conclusions can you draw about advertising claims based on this observation? _____

_____

_____

Now look closely at the pictures that are part of the advertisements. Choose one advertisement and describe the claims that the pictures seem to be making about the product.

_____

_____

_____

Another way to test the claims of advertisers is to read all labels, manuals, or warranties that come with a product. Read them *before* you buy the item! You may also find information that will help you make decisions about *which* product to buy.

Working with a partner, find an owner's manual to study. Then answer the questions below.

1. Which parts of the manual seem most important to you? Explain your answer. _____

_____

2. What is printed in the largest type? _____

_____

3. Why do you think the largest type was used for this particular information? _____

_____

4. What is printed in the smallest type? _____

_____

5. Why do you think this particular information is printed in the smallest type? _____

_____

6. What conclusions can you draw about the purpose of manuals and their relation to advertising? _____

_____

_____

WARRANTIES

Most companies want to stand behind the products they make. They want customers to be happy with their products so that they will buy again or recommend the products to others. As a consumer, you want to be protected against products that are not made well or that do not hold up to ordinary use. To assure consumers that it will stand behind its products, a company makes promises or guarantees that the product will work properly under normal conditions for a certain length of time. These guarantees are called "warranties."

Evaluation

Use the following questions to help you evaluate your performance on this lesson.

❏ Do I consider myself to be a critical reader? Why or why not?

❏ What could I do to become a better critical reader?

❏ What did I find difficult about this lesson? How did I overcome this difficulty?

❏ When working with my partner, did I do my part? What contributions did I make?

BOOKSHELF

You can find many resources in a library or bookstore about consumerism, managing money, and making money, too. The following are just a few examples of the books and magazines that are available. Check with your teacher, librarian, or a local bookstore owner for more titles.

Dollars and Sense: The Teen-Age Consumer's Guide, by Elizabeth McGough.

Smart Spending, by Lois Schmitt.

The Rejects, by Nathan Aaseng.

In Charge: A Complete Handbook for Kids with Working Parents, by Kathy S. Kyte.

Scholastic Choices. A lifestyle magazine for teens by Scholastic, Inc.

Zillions, a magazine for teens by the Consumers Union.

Think about how you spend your money. Then answer the following questions.

1. When you have money, do you spend all of it at one time? _____

_____

2. How do you carry and keep track of the money that you have?

_____

3. Do you save money to buy special things that you want or need? If so, how do you save your money? _____

_____

These questions are about money management. Learning to handle money and planning ahead are important skills for teens to acquire. When you have a job, these skills become very important. When you are independent and living on your own, they become even more important.

People use budgets to help them manage their money. A budget is a written plan for your money. Budgets can help keep you from spending more money than you have. Budgets can also help you to save money.

An expense is something for which you spend money. If you made a list of what you spent money on last month, this would be a list of your expenses.

4. How much money do you usually have to spend each month and from where does it come? _____

_____

5. Think about your expenses for the past month. On what products or services did you spend the most money? _____

_____

Now plan a budget for next month's expenses. Follow these steps to fill in the sample budget on the next page.

1. Choose four categories in which you typically spend the most money every month. Write them in the left column. If you need

to add more rows to the chart, use a separate sheet of paper. All of your monthly expenses should be listed in the chart.

2. In the middle column, list the purchases or products that you need or want to buy next month.

3. In the third column, list how much each purchase costs. Remember that this is a budget for one month. If you buy lunches every school day, then you will need to multiply the cost of one lunch by the number of school days in a month.

4. Finally, add up all the costs and enter the amount in the total box.

CATEGORIES	PURCHASES	COSTS
1.		
2.		
3.		
4.		
5. Miscellaneous		
	TOTAL	

Review your budget. Look at the total at the bottom of column 3. Then answer these questions.

1. Compare the amount of money you actually have with the amount you intend to spend. Will you have enough to cover your expenses next month? _____

2. Will you have any money left over? _____

3. If you answered no to question 1 or 2, what changes can you make in your budget to cover your expenses and have money left over? _____

_____

If you need to, revise your budget now. Make adjustments so that you have *more* than enough money to cover your expenses.

Planning is a very important life skill. It is a skill that involves many other skills. It involves thinking about the future while taking past experiences and present knowledge into account. It involves making predictions about future needs and actions. It also involves understanding actions and their consequences.

Evaluation

Use the following questions to help you evaluate your performance on this lesson.

❏ What did I find difficult about creating a budget?

❏ How well do I manage my money? What grade would I give myself? Why?

❏ Is it important for me to create a budget? Why or why not?

❏ What did I do well in this lesson? What could I have done better?

Making a Decision: Which One to Buy?

Technology has expanded our choices of products and brands. There was a time when the only source of music was a live performance. Today we can listen to music from a wide variety of products, including radio and television, records, cassette tapes, and compact discs. The equipment on which music is played today also comes in many sizes, shapes, and combinations.

In Lesson 1, you learned about some shopping skills. You also inventoried the purchases you made over a month's time, evaluated your shopping decisions, and assessed the choices you made.

In Lesson 2, you examined some advertising claims and identified the facts made in those claims. You also took a critical look at an owner's manual and examined its contents. In Lesson 3, you learned about budgets and how they can help you to manage and save money.

In the unit project, you will identify the reasons that a teen might have for buying a portable radio-cassette player. You will also identify the important features needed in this kind of product. After listing all the options and discussing the pros and cons for each one, you will make a decision about which radio-cassette player you would buy or recommend buying.

STEP 1 Identifying Needs and Features..

In a small group, brainstorm reasons that a teen would want to buy or own a portable radio-cassette player.

Think of as many different reasons as you can. Remember that all ideas are good ones when you are brainstorming. To help prompt ideas, talk about how, when, and where a radio-cassette player might be used. Use the following chart to record the group's ideas. Fill in the left column, User Needs, first.

Product: Portable Radio-Cassette Player

Consumer: Teenagers	Product Features:
User Needs:	

*N*ow think a little harder as you look again at the list. Are there any other reasons or needs that you haven't listed? What about such features as appearance and size? Are these important considerations for a teen?

*R*eview the list of needs. Talk about what features the radio-cassette player should have in order to meet each need. For example, if the user will be carrying it around all day, then the unit would need to be portable and sturdy. Perhaps even a carrying case would be an important feature. If the user wishes to listen to music on the bus, the quality of the earphones would be an important feature. List the desirable features in the right column of the chart.

STEP 2

Researching Available Products

As a group, discuss price limits. If you wish to find the "best" product available, you may not want to set a price limit. Usually, the more expensive radio-cassette players will be ones that appear to be "better" than others. However, they may have many features that make it too expensive for teens. The more expensive items may also have features that you don't want or need. You may, therefore, decide to set a price limit for your search.

Now you need to look at your options. Begin a list of products that have the features you are looking for in a radio-cassette player. Record the information below.

You can use many sources in your search. Look through newspaper advertisements or flyers to see what is currently available. Make notes about prices and specific product names or model numbers, as well as brand names. You might also look through electronics magazines, consumer magazines, or visit an electronics store to see what is available.

Name: ....

Model: ....

Price: ....

Features: ....

STEP 3

Limiting the Options......................

Review your list of products and choose two or three
that best meet the needs you have identified. To help you make a choice,
use the list of needs and features from Step 1, as well as any price limits
you have set. You might also check ratings of different units in consumer
magazines or compare product warranties. Another way to help you limit
the options would be to talk with salespeople. Ask questions about the
various products. For example, you might ask them which radio-cassette
players seem to require the most service, or maintenance.

Circle the two or three products that you chose as the best options.

STEP 4

Making a Decision...............

The final step in this process is to make the best choice. Write the three best options below. Discuss and record the reasons for and against each one.

Option 1		Option 2		Option 3	
Pros	Cons	Pros	Cons	Pros	Cons

*N*ow evaluate the pros and cons and make your decision! Write the name of the product you have chosen: _____

STEP 5

Sharing Your Recommendation............

After your group has agreed on a radio-cassette player, make your recommendation to the class. Support your recommendation with specific reasons. Explain why you chose this particular product and why you think it would be a good choice for teens.

STEP 6

Evaluating the Results...............

As each group makes its recommendation, listen carefully to the reasons for the group's choice. Was the recommendation supported by sound reasons? If different radio-cassette players were recommended, did each product meet the needs of each group? How would you rate your group's ability to make wise decisions about products and services?

1. Circle the incorrect answer. Explain your choice on the lines provided.
   Good money management practices include
   a. planning ahead.   c. impulse buying.
   b. working out a budget.   d. bargain hunting.

   _____

   _____

2. Match each critical thinking skill in Column 1 with the phrase that best describes it
   in Column 2.
   a. making decisions   d. looking for key concepts, facts, opinions, and reasons
   b. reading critically   e. thinking about the future while taking the past and
   c. planning ahead   the present into account
                              f. listing all options, then pros and cons for each option

**Answer the following questions on the lines provided. Use examples and details
to support your answers.**

3. How can people make good decisions when faced with many choices?

   _____

   _____

4. Describe some of the things that you can do to better manage your money.

   _____

   _____

   _____

? **Answer the following essay question on a separate sheet of paper. Support your
answer with examples and details.**

5. Some people claim that advertisements are often written to convince people to buy
   products or services that they really don't want or need. This claim is especially
   true of television commercials and print advertisements that are distributed
   nationally. Do you think this claim is true about advertisements for community
   goods and services? Describe the kind of advertising practices that are used by a
   merchant in your community. Do you think the advertisements are fair? Why or
   why not?

UNIT 6

Making a Difference

Do you believe that you can make a difference in your own or in someone else's life? Making a difference is a real challenge. Think about it. It is easier to stand on the sidelines and watch the game than it is to actually play. It is also easier to watch other people make a difference than it is to make a difference yourself.

There are many ways in which you can make a difference in the lives of people around you. Just take a look. Is there a new student in your class who needs a friend? The student who sits next to you may need help with math homework. Getting involved doesn't only mean big projects, like building shelters for the homeless. There are many projects, big and small, that you can get involved in to help the teens in your community.

In this unit, you'll think critically about becoming involved in your community. You'll observe the teens and problems in your community. You'll learn to research information. You'll also write a summary of your research.

Every community has problems. As a unit project, you'll organize and design a booth for a school or community function. At the booth, your group will distribute information about a problem in your community that affects teens, and you'll try to motivate people to help solve the problem.

81

Saying "NO" to Drugs

Jody

I know firsthand how drugs can hurt someone and destroy a family. My older brother took drugs for almost ten years. He was an alcoholic. I know a lot of people don't think of alcohol as a drug, but it is. And the results can be just as deadly as doing coke or smoking crack.

It took my brother a long time to get the help he needed. Too long. In the process, he did a lot of things he was ashamed of, and he hurt a lot of people, including his family.

Watching Eric waste almost five years of his life inspired me to make sure that other kids don't make the same mistake. I knew they were using drugs, too. What I didn't know was how many other people in our community felt the way I did.

Last semester, I saw an article in a local newspaper about a new program that was starting at the community center. It was for people of all ages who wanted to stop using drugs. I went to the first meeting the following Monday night. I wasn't sure if they would want my help, but I was positive I wanted to do something.

It made me sad to see how few people came to that first meeting. But the head of the group, Mr. McCarthy, said he was sure that would change. First, we had to get out the word. We had to tell people who we were and how we were going to help them help themselves. When he said "we," he looked right at me.

Everyone in the room had a personal reason for being there. We talked about what we had seen in our community and about how much harm drugs had done to the teens who live there. I talked about my brother Eric and his drinking problem. I knew a lot of kids in my school were drinking because they thought it was "safer" than using drugs. They didn't understand what alcohol is and what it can do to your body and mind.

Mr. McCarthy suggested that I help change how kids feel about alcohol. He asked me to write an article for the school paper about the drug program at the community center. He wanted kids to know there were counselors who were available to help them.

I finally wrote that article. Several days later, Mr. McCarthy told me that a couple of students called the substance-abuse hotline number to get information about the drug program. They said that they had gotten the number from my article.

Our program is obviously working. We have ten counselors now. Every month we publish a newsletter with articles about drugs. We want to tell people how dangerous drugs are. We also want them to know where they can get help if they're hooked on drugs.

Maybe you're wondering what we called our group. The name is "Lending a Hand." And we do just that. All of us.

Helping Out With Schoolwork

Darren

I had a lot of trouble when I first learned how to read. But I was lucky. My parents took the time to help me. Now I like school and plan to go on to college when I graduate. I'd like to become a lawyer one day.

Right now, I spend three afternoons a week volunteering in a tutoring program. My school guidance counselor and some of the teachers started the program about a year ago. The program pairs up a younger kid who's having problems in school with an older student.

As soon as I heard about the program, I knew it was something I wanted to do. I can still remember that horrible feeling in the pit of my stomach waiting for a teacher to call on me to read. Even when I knew the answer, I was afraid to raise my hand. I was really self-conscious about reading out loud. And if you don't feel good about yourself in school, you won't feel good about yourself outside of school either.

In our program the volunteers meet with one of our teachers, Ms. Schultz, once a week. We talk about the kids we're tutoring and how we think we can help them. She gives us advice about special books we can use when we tutor.

Personally, I think the word tutor really doesn't describe what goes on in our program. It's a lot more than helping a younger kid with his homework. Because I really like school now, I want to show kids that school can be fun and that it can help them live a better life. I think these kids kind of look up to me now.

I guess the point is that every child needs to have someone who really cares about him. Sure, the tutors help the kids with their homework. But we do more than that. We also try to be positive role models and show the students that we care about what happens to them. Just by listening, we're letting the kids know that they're saying something important.

Actually, I'm probably getting as much or more out of tutoring than the kids I'm working with. I mean, I feel as if I'm doing something worthwhile. **I'm giving something back to people in my community. And that's a good feeling to have.**

TUTOR NEEDED

Good student needed to help sixth grader in math and English.
See Ms. Doma in room 173 for information.

A Community Hotline

Scott

Last year a group of people in our community started a hotline for kids who are in trouble and need someone to talk to. It's not something that started overnight. I mean, there have been lots of articles in the local newspaper about kids who are not attending school and who are just hanging out on the street. A lot of these kids are joining gangs so that they can have the feeling of belonging to something.

There are other problems, too. Some kids are running away from home and trying to live on their own out on the street. For others, life seems to be closing in on them, and they have no one to turn to for help.

Guidance counselors from my high school and two other high schools in our neighborhood got together. They talked to parents and to other city officials who were worried about the kids in the community. They wanted to start a hotline that teens could call any time, night or day, when they are feeling really upset or scared.

The hotline started almost nine months ago. My uncle volunteers one night a week, and he told me what he does. The hotline volunteers let callers know that they aren't alone and that someone else cares and wants to help them. When a teen calls, my uncle gives him or her the names and numbers of other community groups and agencies that can help. Sometimes, talking to a kid who's bummed out is an important first step.

My uncle asked me if I wanted to help out, too. He told me about a training program for hotline volunteers. After you've completed it, you're allowed to answer the phones and counsel the caller.

I was one of the first student volunteers who was trained. The more I found out about what the people here are trying to do, the more excited I became. Instead of putting kids down, the hotline volunteers listen to what callers have to say. No one here passes judgment on what someone else says or does. They just want to make sure that kids get the best help they can when they need it.

To make sure that students know about the hotline and what it does, I talk about our work at different schools in the community. I let teens know that we're not here to get them in trouble. We're here to help them stay out of trouble. I also want kids to know that the identity of anyone who calls the hotline remains confidential. We don't claim to have all the answers, but we can put them on the right track. A lot of times, that's really what someone who's having problems needs.

NATIONAL RUNAWAY HOTLINE
1-800-621-4000

Lesson 1:
Observing Teens in Your Community

Do you take the place in which you live for granted? Do you ever stop and take a good look at your community and the people who live there? What places are there for teens to visit? What interesting teens are there to meet? What problems are there in your community that affect teens? To make a difference in your community, you have to take time to get to know your community and those who live there.

People are what truly make a community unique. Nowhere else in the world will you find an identical mix of nationalities and personalities. Answer the questions below about the teens in your community.

1. What are teens in your community interested in?

_____

_____

2. Where do the teens in your community go for fun?

_____

_____

3. What school and community activities are there for teens to participate in?

_____

_____

4. What problems do teens in your community face?

_____

_____

5. Are teens actively involved in your community? If so, what do they do? If not, why not?

_____

_____

Spend the next several days observing teens in your school and community. Record your observations on the chart on page 86. Add categories to the chart if necessary.

SHOOTING BACK

A problem in many urban communities is the growing number of homeless youths. In 1989, Jim Hubbard, a photojournalist in Washington, D.C., set out to document homelessness in the United States. While he was photographing homeless families, Hubbard discovered a desire among the children to learn photography so that they could show their world and lives in their own unique way.

The children's photographs have been published in a book and can be seen on tour at museums and galleries. Through their pictures, the children have brought the problem of homelessness out of the darkness and have given the homeless faces and names.

Shooting Back has recorded the lives of urban African American children and homeless children in Hawaii and on Native American reservations.

For more information about Shooting Back publications and programs, contact

Shooting Back
1901 18th Street NW
Washington, D.C. 20009
(202) 232-5169

Dress	Activities	Interest
Places	Problems	Other

Every community, whether big or small, has problems to overcome. Many of them directly affect teens. In some communities the problems are violence and drugs. Other communities are struggling with the problem of high unemployment that can also affect a teen's chances for getting an after-school job. Still other communities have serious environmental problems that affect the health of community residents. Use the space below to describe two problems in your community. Explain how these problems affect you or your peers.

_____

_____

_____

_____

DISCUSSION

The world has become smaller because of improved communication and transportation. It is as though we now have one world community rather than distinct, individual communities. Discuss the meaning of a "world community." In what ways are you closer to teens living in other parts of the world? What similarities do you have with teens in other countries? What are the differences? What are the personal advantages and disadvantages of living in a world community?

Evaluation

Use the following questions to help you evaluate your performance on this lesson.

❑ How did this lesson help me to observe my community better?

❑ What did I learn about my community that I didn't know before?

❑ How would I rate my ability as an observer? Why?

86

Lesson 2:
Inquiring About a Topic

In this lesson, you'll become a researcher. You'll research a community problem that affects you or your peers. In a small group, select a topic that is of particular interest to your group or to teens in your community. Possible topics include drug and alcohol addiction, teen pregnancy, gangs, violence, dropping out of school, and homeless teens. Or you might select a topic that you generated in Lesson 1.

Write the topic your group has chosen on the line below.

_____

Before researchers set out to explore their topic, they often generate a list of questions about the topic to help guide their research. As a group, list questions you have about your topic. Write your questions in the following graphic organizer. Then list two possible resources for finding out the answer to each question. If necessary, use a separate sheet of paper to add more questions and sources. Think of questions that will help you to define the problem, identify its causes and effects, and find solutions to the problem.

TIPS ON INTERVIEWING

The following are several tips about conducting an interview:

- **Set up an appointment.** Don't just drop in on the person that you want to interview. Call him or her beforehand to arrange a place and a time to meet. Let the person know the topic of the interview.

- **Be prepared.** Write down your questions before meeting with the person. Make sure that the tape recorder you are using is in good working order and that you have plenty of blank tapes. Be on time for the interview.

- **Be patient.** Give the person whom you are interviewing enough time to think about and answer each question. Don't rush his or her answers.

- **Be polite.** Thank the person for his or her time when the interview is over. Write the person a thank-you note and let him or her read your summary of the interview when it's finished.

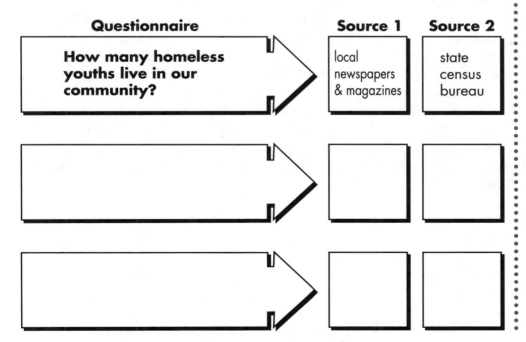

Questionnaire	Source 1	Source 2
How many homeless youths live in our community?	local newspapers & magazines	state census bureau

PRIMARY AND SECONDARY SOURCES

The following are several primary and secondary sources to help you research your topic.

Primary sources include diaries, letters, photographs, printed copies of speeches, personal interviews, and autobiographies.

Secondary sources include textbooks, encyclopedias and other reference books, biographies, and historical fiction. Newspaper and magazine articles can be both primary and secondary sources of information.

Evaluation

Use the following questions to help you evaluate your performance on this lesson.

❑ What did I find to be the most difficult part of my research? How did I overcome this difficulty?

❑ What process did I use to decide on the topic of my research?

❑ What skills did I develop as I completed this lesson?

❑ Now that I have practiced interviewing, what changes would I make in the interview I conducted?

Next, select the questions that you will answer and begin your research. A good place to start doing research is at the library. The library contains both primary and secondary sources of information. Read about the differences between primary and secondary sources in the sidenote. Look for newspaper and magazine articles that relate to your topic. There may also be audiotapes and video clips that you will find useful.

Another way of gathering information is to interview people in your community. For example, if your topic is dropping out of school, you may wish to interview your school's guidance counselor. Write the names of the people whom you would like to interview on a separate sheet of paper.

When interviewing someone, it is important to be prepared for the interview. Read the sidenote about interviewing on page 87. Below, write five questions that you are going to use in your interview.

1. _____
2. _____
3. _____
4. _____
5. _____

Rather than write down everything that is said during the interview, get permission to tape-record your conversation. By using a tape recorder you can play back your interview at a later time and review the information that is most helpful to you.

Another way to gather information about your topic is by watching news reports on television. You may be surprised to find out that the topic of your research is not an isolated problem. Teens all over the country and the world are facing many of the same problems that teens in your community face.

Local community-service organizations may also help you with your research. Each organization usually focuses on one particular problem. Find out which organizations and agencies might help you in your research and write the names, addresses, and phone numbers below.

_____ _____
_____ _____
_____ _____
_____ _____

Lesson 3:
Evaluating Sources of Information

Researchers and critical thinkers understand that not all resources are reliable. Just because something is in print or because someone says that something is true, doesn't mean that the information is factual or correct. You have to check facts and evaluate the source of your information.

One way to evaluate a source's reliability is to fact check. If more than one source says the same thing, most likely the information is reliable. Another way to evaluate a source is to check it against a set of criteria that you establish. In the chart below, write the criteria by which you will evaluate a source's reliability. Write a set of criteria for each type of resource you use.

People
Television
Print Information
Other

Once you have established the criteria, use them to evaluate whether each source you consult will be accurate and reliable.

To **evaluate** means to judge or to determine the worth of something. In this case, you are judging, or evaluating, the accuracy and reliability of your sources of information.

CRITERIA

Criteria are the standards by which something is to be evaluated. They are the characteristics that any given thing must have. In this case, you are writing the characteristics that each source must have before you can judge it to be accurate and reliable.

Evaluation

Use the following questions to help you evaluate your performance on this lesson.

❑ What process did I use to establish the criteria I used to judge a source's reliability?

❑ Were the majority of my sources reliable? Why or why not?

❑ How would I rate my ability to evaluate sources of information?

Lesson 4:
Synthesizing Information

To synthesize means to "combine parts or elements to form a whole." In Lesson 2, you researched a topic of your choice. In this lesson, you'll identify all the parts of your research and organize your information in outline form. Then you'll synthesize these parts into a summary. In other words, you'll combine all the parts, or elements, of your research to form a whole.

Once researchers have gathered their information, they usually write a summary. This summary synthesizes their research and answers five basic questions: Why? Where? Who? What? and So what? Use the outline below to synthesize and organize your research.

TOPIC: _____

I.   Why is the topic that I selected important?

       A.

       B.

       C.

II.   Where is the problem most common?

       A.

       B

       C.

III.   Who is most affected by this problem?

       A.

       B.

       C.

IV.   What are the major aspects of the problem?

       A.

       B.

       C.

V.   What are some possible solutions?

       A.

       B.

       C.

Now that you have completed an outline of your summary, it's time to write. Imagine that you are informing an organization, agency, or political leader about your chosen community problem. Write your summary in the form of a business letter. Use the space below for your letter. Use additional paper, if necessary.

heading ▶ _____
_____
date ▶ _____

_____
_____ ◀ inside address
_____

_____, ◀ salutation

body ▶ _____
_____
_____
_____
_____
_____
_____
_____
_____
_____
_____
_____

closing ▶ _____,
_____

BOOKSHELF

You can find many resources in a library or bookstore about people who have made a difference. The following are just a few of the books that are available. Check with your teacher, librarian, or a local bookstore owner for more titles.

Kids With Courage: True Stories about Young People Making a Difference, by Barbara A. Lewis.

Making a Difference: The Story of an American Family, by Margaret Hodges.

Biography Today: Profiles of People of Interest to Young Readers, by Laurie L. Harris.

Evaluation

Use the following questions to help you evaluate your performance on this lesson.

❏ What part of my research was the most useful in writing my summary?

❏ How useful was the outline in helping me to organize my research?

❏ How did this lesson help me to develop the skill of synthesizing?

How You Can Make a Difference

How often do you hear someone say, "Well, I'd like to get involved, but what can one person do?" One person can do much more than you think. Many programs for teens were started by one person who took a stand on an issue and became involved in trying to solve a problem.

In Lesson 1, you looked more closely at your community and the teens who live there. You probably learned something about your community that you never knew before. In Lesson 2, you selected one community problem that affects teens. You asked questions about the problem and conducted research on it. In Lesson 3, you evaluated your sources of information. Finally, in Lesson 4, you wrote a business letter in which you synthesized the information that you discovered during your research.

For the unit project, you'll share information about your chosen problem with the community. You'll design a booth and distribute information about the problem you've chosen, and you will try to get the community involved in solving the problem.

Brainstorming Ideas...............................

With the help of your teacher, divide into small groups according to the topic you researched for Lesson 2. As a group, brainstorm ways in which you can communicate information to the community about the problem you researched. These ideas will become the components that you will have at your booth. Think about posters, brochures, videotapes, and so on. Use the space below to record your ideas. Remember that during any brainstorming, all suggestions are accepted. Later on, you will evaluate which ideas will be most effective.

_____ _____ _____

_____ _____ _____

STEP 2

Evaluating Ideas.................

Evaluate each idea from Step 1. Rate each idea from one to six, with 1 being the most effective way to communicate information. Use the lines below to rank your group's ideas.

1. _____
2. _____
3. _____
4. _____
5. _____
6. _____

Next, the group needs to decide what information will be presented in each component and which component each member will be responsible for. As an example, if one student is responsible for developing a video and another is responsible for writing a brochure, you need to determine what information will go into each component. Perhaps the video will show the problem and the brochure will provide background and statistics about the problem. A third component could then propose solutions to the problem. Use the following questions as a guideline for developing each piece that you will present at your booth.

1. What is the problem?
2. What are the causes of the problem?
3. What attempts have been made to solve the problem? What possible solutions are there that haven't been tried yet?

STEP 3

Developing and Writing Materials.................................

Using the research you conducted in Lesson 2, write the components that you will display in your booth. As you develop your materials, you may decide that you need to conduct more research. Be sure you allow enough time for additional research.

STEP 4

Finding Solutions......................................

Use the following graphic organizer to help you to establish the problem, the causes of the problem, and possible solutions.

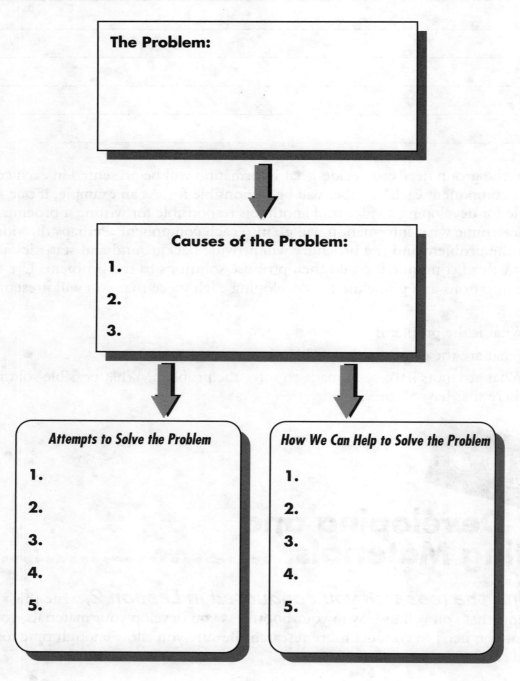

The Problem:

Causes of the Problem:

1.

2.

3.

Attempts to Solve the Problem

1.

2.

3.

4.

5.

How We Can Help to Solve the Problem

1.

2.

3.

4.

5.

Perhaps the most important purpose for your booth is to motivate people in your community to become part of the solution. Spend time now in making sure that the materials you developed have steps that the public can take to help solve the problem. Use the following questions as a guideline for evaluating your solutions:

1. Is the solution realistic?
2. Will the solution be effective in solving the problem? Why or why not?
3. Can the community easily become involved in the solution? Why or why not?

STEP 5

Sharing Information and Solutions

As a class, decide how best to organize the sharing of your information with the community. You might, for example, organize a school fair whose theme is "We Can Make a Difference!" You might decide to set up one or more booths at several school functions, such as basketball and volleyball games. You might also suggest that the principal set up a school assembly to which you invite the community.

STEP 6

Evaluating the Project

One way to evaluate the effectiveness of your group's information is to have an evaluation form that people who visit your booth can complete. Develop a one-page questionnaire for people to fill out before leaving your booth. You might, for example, use the following questions:

- What information was most helpful in defining the problem we presented?
- What information was most helpful in proposing solutions to the problem?
- What new information did you learn about the problem?
- What did you like most about our booth?
- What did you like least or what do we need to improve?
- Did our materials challenge you to make a difference in our community? Why or why not?
- Are you planning to become actively involved in the solution of the problem? Explain your answer.

1. State whether the following statement is true or false and explain your answer on the lines provided. Learning more about your community helps you make a difference in your city or town.

_____

_____

2. Complete the following statement and explain your answer on the lines provided. I can make a difference in my community by

_____

_____

Answer the following questions on the lines provided. Use examples and details to support your answers.

3. What steps can you take to learn more about a teen problem in your community?

_____

_____

_____

_____

4. Why is synthesizing an important skill to use when you research a topic?

_____

_____

_____

_____

? Answer the following essay question on a separate sheet of paper. Support your answer with examples and details.

5. Every community is filled with people who are making a difference. Name one person in your community whom you admire for making a difference. What do you admire most about this person? How does this person encourage you to get more involved in your community?